p entrepreneurs' passion for their 'killer app' is often only ed by disappointment and failure. Any 'great idea' will only t is met with customer enthusiasm. *The Power of Pull* pro- a roadmap for resolving this conundrum, explaining why few succeed and showing how to engage customers to turn ppointment into opportunity."

—John Seddon, managing director,
Vanguard Consulting

Praise fo

The Power o

"If you don't know why people buy things, y
to sell . . . but you also don't know what to buil
gives you a theory that solves this."

—Bob Moesta, author of *Deman*

"This is how we built CloudLock from zero to a $29
tion in a few years. Now as VCs, it's how the teams w
go from ideas to millions in revenue in months."

—Ron Zalkind, founding general partner, Lama

"A bracing, essential corrective to startup mythology—
Snyder replaces wishful thinking with the blunt mechanics
what actually makes customers buy, told with hard-won clarity."

—Tom Eisenmann, professor of entrepreneurship, Harvard Business School

"Rob's ideas have given our founders an unfair advantage as they navigate from idea to scale. Every early-stage founder should read this book."

—Gaurav Jain, cofounder and managing partner, Afore Capital

"Before they can get to repeatable sales, founders need to find a repeated, intense need. *The Power of Pull* is your guide to finding that intense need and fitting a product to it. After that, you're off to the races."

—Peter Kazanjy, author of *Founding Sales*

THE POWER OF PULL

THE POWER OF PULL

What You Need to Know About Customer Demand to Build a Successful Startup (and Why Most Founders Get It Wrong)

ROB SNYDER

New York

Cover design by Kapo Ng
Cover image © Amine Chakour / Shutterstock.com

Basic Venture
Hachette Book Group
1290 Avenue of the Americas, New York, NY 10104
www.basic-venture.com

Printed in the United States of America

First Edition: July 2026

Published by Basic Venture, an imprint of Hachette Book Group, Inc.
The Basic Venture name and logo is a registered trademark of the Hachette Book Group.

Print book interior design by Bart Dawson.

Library of Congress Control Number: 2026938707

ISBNs: 9781541705951 (hardcover), 9781541705968 (ebook)

LSC-C

Printing 1, 2026

To Grace

CONTENTS

THE POWER OF PULL

INTRODUCTION

DEMAND IS ALL YOU NEED

Two weeks after I graduated from Harvard Business School, venture capital investors wired over $1 million into my startup's bank account. It was time to scale.

My small team and I felt *over*prepared, if anything. We'd started with a massive vision to transform the multibillion-dollar workforce management software industry. We'd done months of market research across restaurants, warehouses, janitorial firms, security firms, you name it. We'd conducted hundreds of customer interviews. We did competitive analyses and were convinced that there was a big problem to be solved, a massive market opportunity, and a differentiated product direction. We ran validation experiments, actively attempting to disprove our business hypotheses. With no budget, we had even built a software platform and had multiple businesses piloting our workforce management software. Their usage patterns and testimonials suggested we were onto something big.

We had, of course, devoured every book, blog, and podcast on entrepreneurship we could get our hands on. I took every available startup class at Harvard and spent every moment outside of class in Harvard's startup studio, the Innovation Lab. I recruited a group of advisors who had brought companies from zero to millions in revenue and sold their successful companies for hundreds of millions of dollars.

Now, with cash in the bank, it was "go" time.

Guess what happened next?

We spent the next two years getting repeatedly punched in the face, unable to convince a single customer to buy and use our product.

As a result, we pivoted the business multiple times, testing different permutations of our product in different market segments. Each time, we were confident that *this time* we'd done it right. And each time, an indifferent world taught us we were wrong. It felt like we were pushing a product the market *should* want but didn't. No matter how much research we did, how many cold calls I did, how much value we promised, or how hard we pushed and persuaded . . . customers didn't bite.

How could this happen to us? We'd worked nonstop, built by the book. Despite all this, we had nothing to show. Worse, we couldn't understand *why* our business wasn't working. Did we have the wrong product? The wrong sales approach? The wrong target market? The wrong messaging? The wrong team? Or were we just incompetent?

On top of that, we couldn't tell how far away we were from figuring our business out. Were we one small tweak away from hypergrowth? Or were we totally lost and backward?

Our problems felt unsolvable. There were infinite possible reasons our business wasn't working. And infinite possible solutions. The internet and our advisors offered never-ending pieces of conflicting advice, each of which sounded right. Resulting in, of course, an endless list of things we could do and probably a trillion permutations of a business that could theoretically work.

My brain ground to a halt. I couldn't figure it out. I couldn't understand how anyone could figure this out. In my happiest moments, I felt like a fraud and a failure. Don't ask me about my less-happy moments.

I was in what I now call the "pain cave." It's where we entrepreneurs go when plan A doesn't work. We suffer in the pain cave as plans B, C, D . . . and, eventually, Z also don't work. In the pain cave, we struggle to understand why nobody seems to want our product. We stare market indifference in the face and aren't sure how to change the market's mind. There are so many things that could work—should work—yet somehow we can't find one thing that really does work in practice.

Leaving aside the lucky few entrepreneurs who catch lightning in a bottle, *everyone* spends time in the pain cave. A lucky few escape. But most give up here and get a "real" job.

Two years into my personal pain cave, I was ready to give up. By then, many of my entrepreneur friends had packed it in. They seemed to be enjoying their corporate jobs and cushy salaries. Anything seemed better than the pain cave; I clearly didn't have whatever it takes to start a company.

And then something strange happened.

One day, a prospective customer—an owner of forty franchise restaurants—called me. He had reacted unenthusiastically to my sales pitch a few months earlier. This time, he said, "Hey Rob, I know you're a tech guy. Can you help me solve this hiring issue I've got?"

The challenge: Our product had nothing to do with hiring restaurant employees, and I knew exactly nothing about the topic. The restaurant owner only called me because he remembered me as a computer nerd. He didn't want the product I'd pitched to him at all. Still, I was so deep in the pain cave, and this was the first instance of genuine customer interest I'd experienced in two years, that I said, "Sure, I'll figure something out for you."

In a few hours, I built a very ugly, low-tech solution to his hiring problem. He liked it. I showed other restaurant owners what we'd done for him. They liked it too. In a few months, we went from zero to $100,000 in revenue. In a year, we were at $1 million. Within two years of that fateful phone call, we were at $4 million in revenue.

It worked, which was nice. But I was still miserable because I couldn't understand *why* it worked.

Clearly, we had gone from "building something that *nobody* wanted" to "building something that people *really* wanted." It was as if our product went from "forgettable" to "irresistible." But I couldn't figure out *what exactly had changed.* I knew that prospective customers now leaned in and bought when I talked, rather than zoning out and ignoring my follow-up messages. Yet everything else about our business—from our website, to our hastily built product (which actually started as a spreadsheet, not a "real" software product), to our sales pitch—was *objectively worse* than the well-researched, thoughtfully crafted things we'd built previously. More concerning, we hadn't followed any of the best practices we'd been taught. There was zero plan or process. The business just seemed to emerge over time after we figured out what one customer, then the next, then the next, wanted.

At first, I thought our case was a fluke, that we just got lucky, that we were succeeding despite doing things the wrong way.

But then I talked with other founders who'd recently emerged from their pain caves and heard their behind-the-scenes stories. Our journey wasn't an anomaly after all. Many founders I spoke to also felt like they had broken the rules, like they had succeeded despite not operating by the book. I now believe these startups escaped the pain cave because they threw the books away.

These founders' startup outcomes weren't identical; some had scaled to billion-dollar exits, others had been acquired for a few million dollars. Still others had found initial traction but hit difficult times and closed their companies down. Despite this, everyone's path *out* of the pain cave was shockingly similar and oddly simple.

As I heard their stories, I grew obsessed with trying to understand exactly what causes startups to work. What's happening behind the scenes at the moment a startup takes off? How do we build something people truly want, and why does this seemingly simple task wind up being so difficult? What causes prospective customers to look at a company's product or service and say, "Oh my gosh, where have you been all my life?" and immediately buy it? Why does traditional startup advice sound right but seem not to work? And how do we operate confidently in the face of so much ambiguity?

I spent years interviewing over one thousand entrepreneurs who navigated the pain cave. I analyzed over three thousand different recorded sales and postsales conversations from companies selling everything from consumer products to cryptocurrency infrastructure. I joined as an advisor or fractional executive with over a dozen startups to help them get out of the pain cave and get to at least $1 million in revenue. And I've continued building my own startups, navigating the pain cave as many times as I possibly can. As my patient wife will attest, this obsession is much to the detriment of my physical and mental well-being. But hey, you get a book out of it.

What I've learned firsthand and from serial founders looks and feels wildly different from what you've been taught in business school or popular entrepreneurship books. It might break your brain like it broke mine. And then it will likely save you months or years in the pain cave as you navigate your startup journey.

DEMAND COMES FIRST

This book makes one central argument: Entrepreneurship does not require the fancy presentations, mounds of venture capital funding, business plans, endless market research and analysis, or scientific-seeming experiments we've been told are necessary by seemingly every academic, influencer, investor, and commentator on Earth. The latest ninety-four-step entrepreneurship process or ivory tower framework is more likely to prevent entrepreneurial success than cause it. And the fancy theories by academics, venture capital investors, and even successful entrepreneurs fail to capture the simple process by which startups come to life.

There are many reasons startups fail, but there is only one reason they succeed. *New ventures succeed if, and only if, they find and serve customer demand.* No matter what else they do right, they can't succeed if they don't find and serve demand. If there's no demand, the entrepreneur can push as hard as he wants—but buyers won't buy.

Unfortunately, we're never taught *what demand is.* We tend to think demand means "people who want our product"—which sounds right but leads us straight to the pain cave. Demand has nothing to do with our product. *Instead, the simplest way to think about demand is that it's "the top priority on a buyer's to-do list, right now."* This priority is about accomplishing something in her life; it is not about wanting products or buying anything. In other words: Demand is not "wanting supply." If a buyer has bad options to get her priority done, and our product "fits" better, she will buy it. If not, she won't. We can't force her to buy our product, and we don't control her to-do list. Her demand—and demand generally—exists whether or not our business exists.

When we find demand, our startups tend to take off. That's because when we find demand, it feels like buyers are *pulling* the product out of our hands, rather than us *pushing* the product into theirs. When we try to push our product into their hands, we're fighting against their to-do list, attempting to persuade them that they should prioritize something other than what they're focused on right now. It would be weird if this worked. If it did work, somebody would have to say, "OK, I'm going to drop all my projects and priorities to buy your product!" Which, of course, has never been said.

On the other hand, when buyers have demand, they say things like: "You found me at the perfect time!" "I'm actually working on this right now!" "Have you been listening in on our meetings?" "This is exactly what I've been looking for." "Can I bring my whole team to see this tomorrow?" When customers pull like this, we need to do very little convincing, and our businesses tend to grow very fast.

We're traditionally taught to push our product rather than to find pull. It's our job, we're told, to identify a huge market, craft a big vision, convince everyone they should want our product by poking and prodding at their pain points, and then unveil some sort of irresistible offer to drive urgency. When we do this, buyers tune us out. Because they don't care about what we think they should want. Frankly, they don't care about us at all—they care about themselves.

Demand thinking embraces this cold reality. Buyers couldn't care less about our vision for how the world should work. They don't care if we've identified a big market gap. They don't care about our "game-changing" technology. They don't care if we offer an attractive return on investment (ROI). They don't want us tickling their pain points and problems, most of which they won't ever address. They will never wake up in the morning and say, "You know what? Today's the day I'm really hankering for a new Enterprise Resource Planning software module."

We can try to convince potential customers that they're wrong and we're right—if we want to spend the rest of our lives smashing our head against the walls of the pain cave. Because given what's on most people's to-do lists, *it would be weird if they bought our product*. They're not going to drop their priorities even if our product would benefit them or fix their pain points. Demand thinking, on the other hand, acknowledges that buyers have meaningful things they're trying to do in their lives. If we can help them accomplish whatever they're trying to do, they might pull. If not, we're an annoying, pushy distraction, no matter how shiny and technologically impressive our product is.

Demand is a startup's first bottleneck. When we understand demand, we understand what *causes* buyers to buy our product. When we find and serve demand, it *causes* our startup to take off. If we don't find demand, nothing else we do matters.

But demand has always been an ambiguous, amorphous concept—if it's talked about at all. We are taught to ask questions like: What do buyers want? What are the problems they're trying to solve? What are buyers' jobs to be done? These point us in roughly the right direction but aren't specific enough. We come up with imprecise, hand-wavy answers like, "Buyers are trying to hit their revenue goals," and then go back to pushing our product and suffering.

To make demand concrete, I've created the PULL framework. While the word *pull* is usually used as a verb (i.e., buyers *pull* the product out of our hands), I use PULL (all caps) in this book as a noun to refer to the framework.

There are four components of PULL. Buyers have PULL if they have (1) a *project* on their to-do list that's (2) *unavoidable* right now, and they consider (3) a *list* of one or multiple options for completing their project, but they think their options have serious (4) *limitations*. The framework:

P	U	L	L
A buyer has a **PROJECT** on their to-do list	that's **UNAVOIDABLE** right now.	They consider a **LIST** of options to get the project done	but they think their options have serious **LIMITATIONS**.

PULL—an unavoidable project with unworkable options for getting it done—defines a gap: a space where a new product can succeed. Our startup's product—our *supply* to buyers' *demand*—needs to "fit" the buyers' PULL. Simply put: Our product just needs to help them accomplish their project where their existing options fall short. Buyers don't care how technologically sophisticated our product is or whether it was made by elves; they care about their PULL. If our product fits, they will *pull* it out of our hands. If not, we push. More bluntly: *When a buyer doesn't have PULL, it would be weird if he bought our product. When a buyer does have PULL, it would be weird if he didn't buy our product (so long as it fits his PULL).*

So yeah. PULL is the most important thing. The primary job of a startup founder is to find PULL and design around it. But how? This is difficult but not complicated.

Entrepreneurs start with a PULL hypothesis: We bet that this person has PULL right now and therefore will pull our product out of our hands.

We then use this PULL hypothesis to try to sell and deliver. The PULL framework, it turns out, is a wildly helpful sales framework. Entrepreneurs use it to structure their sales conversations, describe their products clearly, and diagnose root causes when potential customers don't buy.

But because the world is complicated and messy, our PULL hypothesis is almost always wrong on day one. So, as we try to sell to early customers, we watch for which customers *pull the hardest* before and after they buy. These customers buy fast as if our product is irresistible, and they use the product after they've purchased it as if they're addicted. I call this kind of customer a "hell yes" customer. By observing these customers, the entrepreneur can iterate from their initial PULL hypothesis to a fast-growing business built around real PULL.

Bringing it all together: A startup is the combination of demand (PULL) and supply (how the startup serves PULL). Put these two things together and you get a *repeatable customer success story*. This is the story of a single customer who had intense demand, who pulled hard. It explains how the entrepreneur's supply fits the buyer's demand. And critically, this story is repeatable—while the story is about one customer, it is relevant to many similar customers. The repeatable success story looks like this:

Repeatable Success Story Jane, Director of Human Resources at Acme Corp		
Demand or Supply	**Component**	**Success Story**
Demand	Project	Jane was trying to accomplish this project: _____.
	Unavoidable	This project was unavoidable because Jane was in this situation: __________.
	List of options	Jane considered these options to accomplish her project: __________.
	Limitations	She perceived her options to have these serious limitations: __________.
Supply	What we offer	Jane chose to work with us because we offered: __________________.
	Results	As a result, Jane was able to: __________.

When potential customers see this success story, they understand what the entrepreneur is selling and why people like them buy it, which means an entrepreneur can use her success story as her primary marketing and sales collateral. If the entrepreneur truly understands the elements of her customer success story, every potential customer pulls upon seeing the success story, and the business grows fast as a result.

All entrepreneurs need, then, is to find PULL and craft one repeatable customer success story. Once they've done this, growing the business is simply a matter of repeating this one success story.

Unfortunately, our brains are so polluted by convoluted, academic approaches to entrepreneurship that this simplicity can be counterintuitive and even off-putting. We simply assume that the early stage of startups is so mystical, so failure prone, so difficult, that it cannot possibly be governed by something as straightforward as PULL, or as simple as one repeatable customer success story. How did we get it so backward?

HOW DID WE GET HERE?

As entrepreneurship has gotten more popular, the entrepreneurial process has somehow gotten more complicated. Decades ago, entrepreneurship was for dweebs and dropouts. They didn't have playbooks, frameworks, or even language to describe what they were doing. These old-school entrepreneurs did the obvious, practical things to not die: sell, serve, repeat. They were left alone by the business elite, who preferred politicking their way up the corporate ladder, shooting for partnership status in a consulting firm, or joining a top hedge fund. One of my mentors, a Harvard Business School (HBS) graduate from the early 1990s, told me that there were no entrepreneurship courses at HBS when he was a student. When he started a technology company, his peers scratched their heads: Why would he do this and make $80,000 per year when he could make $300,000, plus bonus, plus fly first class? (When he later sold his business for over $350 million dollars, everyone said they always knew he'd be successful and that they had always been interested in technology startups.)

Entrepreneurship became interesting due to a variety of factors. Most importantly, elite corporate jobs, as well as those in consulting and investing, are hell. Long hours, office politics, nonstop meetings, layoffs, restructurings, cubicles, HR departments, soulless drudgery. Finally, there was a viable alternative: Nerds became dot-com millionaires, and entrepreneurship became cool. Then came the meteoric rise of Facebook and the Web 2.0 behemoths, Salesforce.com and software-as-a-service, Uber and the online marketplaces, and (perhaps temporarily) cryptocurrency millionaires. With fun offices, sky-high profit margins, unicorns popping up every day, zero interest rates, hoodie dress codes, and skyrocketing interest in venture capital as an asset class, the business elite turned their eyes toward startups.

And as startups got hot, everyone wanted to know the secret to startup success. A whirlwind of advice emerged. From "get rich quick" gurus selling snake oil, to academics trying to parse out what makes ventures succeed or fail, to accelerators promising to kick-start new ventures, to movies like *The Social Network* and widely popular entrepreneurial bibles like *The Lean Startup, The Hard Thing About Hard Things, The Mom Test,* and *Four Steps to the Epiphany,* the airwaves filled with startup advice and lore.

I have consumed virtually every piece of advice out there, and *nothing* sufficiently emphasizes the primacy of demand or deeply explores how demand works. Perhaps this is because most entrepreneurial advice seems to be based on chronicling and reverse-engineering why a startup succeeded *after* they succeeded. And when you look at startups after they're successful, it sure appears as if *people want their product* or as if *their product is irresistible.* Demand, of course, is the invisible force that makes this happen. But because it's invisible, demand is either ignored or misunderstood—to every entrepreneur's detriment.

An analogy: Imagine an apple falling from a tree. It sure appears as if that apple wants to be on the ground. Yet we would be sent straight to a psychiatrist for claiming that the reason the apple fell from the tree was that the apple "had pain points and problems in the tree" or "the ground offered compelling ROI." No! Obviously, gravity caused the apple to fall. It is the same thing with demand: It's invisible and causal. Yet unlike gravity, demand is not commonly understood. As a result, modern entrepreneurship advice essentially tells us to lecture apples about their pain points to get them to fall from the tree. It doesn't work, and we look quite foolish when we try.

Because nobody focuses on demand, everyone misses the causal force behind startup success. Therefore, we entrepreneurs do customer interviews without knowing what we're looking for—and we find things that seem important but aren't. We run poorly designed experiments that test irrelevant hypotheses. We follow sales methodologies from big companies, but it's not obvious whether the sales methodology is causing or inhibiting the big company's success. All in all, these practices might barely work if we get lucky and stumble across PULL. Obviously, this is rare: How likely are we to find something we don't know we're supposed to look for?

As a result, the startup world is largely rudderless. And founders try to navigate this fog with never-ending, counterproductive planning and pseudoscientific research. And a heck of a lot of pretending.

Three stories show us the sorry state of entrepreneurship:

LARPING

Ish's first startup launched with fanfare. Four brutal years later, the business died with a whimper.

Which was shocking, because Ish had done everything right. He'd gone through Y Combinator, the legendary startup accelerator. He'd raised millions of dollars from prominent investors on a big idea. He'd hired top software engineers and was building fast in an exciting direction. Ish isn't an idiot, either: He was a high-performing engineer at Facebook, was recognized on Forbes's 30 Under 30 list, and helped run the University of Michigan's data structure and algorithms course while he received his master's in computer science.

So what happened?

As Ish reflects on what went wrong, he sums it up in one sentence: "I was LARPing and didn't realize it." LARPing, if you're unfamiliar with the term, stands for "live action role-playing." It's the activity where adults pretend they are, for example, medieval knights and stage elaborate faux battles in the woods with wooden swords. Though it's not how I spend my weekends, I have nothing against LARPing in the woods. But when founders LARP, our businesses fail. We *pretend* to build a business, instead of actually building a business. Perhaps we spend months perfecting our mission, brand, and social impact statement. Or we spend our precious time and money building a product that fits our vision of how the world should work. We fall in love with lofty ideas—like "solving climate change"—instead of falling in love with helping customers. Often we speak at entrepreneurship events, go to startup conferences, spend time in strategy meetings, hire agencies to get press coverage, plan company offsites, start podcasts, do land acknowledgments, and compete in pitch competitions.

Nobody sets out to LARP, of course. We don't realize we're LARPing. The things we're doing all *seem* important. They are often things that successful entrepreneurs do after they are successful. Before we have a successful business, it feels like there is an infinite number of things we need to do to create a successful business. Why not play Whac-A-Mole trying to complete the million different priorities we're told are important by startup advisors, social media influencers, academic methodologies, and the revisionist histories of successful companies?

Unfortunately, we can waste a lot of time LARPing. We can spend months or years playing pretend while thinking we're building a real business. We can follow methodologies that tell us we're doing the right thing, despite us delaying selling to and serving customers. We can LARP for ninety-hour workweeks, burning ourselves out without realizing we've been acting like absolute fools.

LARPing might seem crazy, but it's exactly how we've been taught to think about entrepreneurship. Media outlets show entrepreneurs blathering on at conferences, not grinding away responding to customer support tickets. Add onto this all the entrepreneurship books, business school courses, and online influencers that suggest our primary purpose is something other than serving customers—seeing into the future, saving the whales, building a product we envision the world should want, emulating some funhouse-mirror version of Steve Jobs.

The same thing happens every time I speak at an entrepreneurship event: I make the blatantly obvious claim that if we don't primarily focus on finding PULL and serving customers our businesses won't survive. And I always get pearl-clutching pushback. "But we have a mission *everyone* should care about!" says one entrepreneur. "Customers don't really know what they want. It's our job to show them what they should want!" "Henry Ford said we shouldn't build faster horses!" says another.

While reality will eventually kick these entrepreneurs in the teeth, I occasionally respond: "Cool, but remember: Nobody cares about you, your product, your goals, your mission, your vision, or how you think the world should work. They care about themselves and getting through their day. Your business is dead by default, and the only way to not die is to generate revenue from customers. To do that, you have to figure out how to serve them, not try to convince them to worship you." For some entrepreneurs in the audience, this helps them snap out of LARPing mode. Most of the time, I don't get invited back.

Ish's point about LARPing hits me particularly hard. I spent years LARPing without realizing it. When I realized what I'd been doing, I felt betrayed. Overwhelmed. Furious. Embarrassed. I had wasted years of my life under the assumption that I was doing the "right" things to build my startup. I'd worked really hard and accomplished less than nothing. And now, I had to figure it all out from scratch.

I was lucky because my startup still had cash in the bank. Founders often realize they've been LARPing too late to save their businesses. They've already spent most of their time and money on everything but serving customers and, with a few months of cash left, slowly realize that finding demand is all that really matters. At that point, they're screwed. They usually can't raise more money. In the end, those startups die with a reality-distorting social media epitaph: "I'm proud of the team and product we built; the market just wasn't ready for it." Sure.

As I write this, Ish is building his second company. This time, he is entirely focused on serving customers. Ish generated more revenue in the first year of his new business than his last company's four years combined. Then he generated more new revenue in *one month* than in his first year. No, his success isn't guaranteed. But he's not LARPing, so his failure isn't guaranteed either.

PLANNING THE UNPLANNABLE

Varsha wasn't sure whether she was in the pain cave or not. She had found some success with her software startup Offstream, which was now earning over $100,000 in annual revenue. But it wasn't playing out exactly like she'd planned during her Harvard MBA. She was selling a combination of a product and a consulting service because that's what customers would buy, but Varsha's plan for the business was to only sell software, not consulting, because consulting wasn't as scalable as software. In her mind, if the business needed to be all software at step 10, why wouldn't it be all software at step 1? Varsha also worried that her customers were all in a tiny, tiny niche—biochar project developers—of which there were maybe three hundred potential customers in the world. Varsha knew that, in order to grow big, she had to expand her market. But how?

Varsha's story is common. We often start out with grand plans to attack big markets with scalable products. *We do this because we think we need to plan big and plan for scale.* When we do find PULL, it's always with one person, who almost always represents a small niche and a not-so-scalable offering. And we feel conflicted because on the one hand, it's nice to have actual customers, while on the other hand, it's unclear how *where we are today* gets to *where we want to be in a few years.* We think there's something wrong with us: We just haven't planned, white-boarded, or analyzed enough. Another friend got stuck at $1 million in revenue in a never-ending cycle of vision documents and strategy retreats, desperate to answer the unanswerable question: Now that we're at step 1, what does step 10 look like?

We book-reading entrepreneurs tend to be overthinkers. We want to be able to analyze things at our desks, follow a process to construct a plan, and then work very hard to implement our plan. This is the recipe for success in school and most of the working world. And we tend to believe that the entrepreneurial world works like this too. In fact, because entrepreneurship is risky and uncertain, we think we need more research, analysis, and planning to validate that we are headed in the right direction. When we get information that doesn't align with our research and plans, we get disoriented. I spent countless hours locked in a conference room, trying to craft a multiyear roadmap that made sense and led to a billion-dollar company. I emerged, exhausted, with a logically sound and rigorous plan that didn't stand a chance in reality. And each time my plan hit the wall, I went back and locked myself in that conference room. *This time I'll get it right,* I thought, every time.

Reality hit me after speaking with a bunch of early-stage venture capital investors. They invest when companies are small and usually have no traction. If anyone could see the future, it would be these investors. I asked each investor, "How can you tell in advance if a startup will be big?"

One young investor, a few years into his investing experience, gave the acceptable MBA-logic response. He walked me through, in detail, how he assessed each investment. He explained the math behind his approach: Early-stage startups obey a power-law distribution, where some become billion-dollar companies but most fail. In order to earn a good return as an investor, you have to swing for a billion-dollar outcome in every investment. Obviously, he had to figure out which of his potential investments were most likely to get to over $100 million in annual revenue in the next eight to ten years. So he grilled the founders of every potential investment on their revenue projections, their beachhead market, their product roadmap, and their competition. This made sense to me at the time.

Then I talked to an old, crotchety computer nerd who had put the first money into several billion-dollar unicorns and 10-billion-dollar "decacorns" over his decades of investing. Annoyed with my question, he threw up his hands and said, "Honestly, Rob, I don't have a damn clue. I never know who's going to be successful in advance. Everything changes. It starts as a little tool for some tiny part of the market, and in a couple of years, if the founders are any good, they figure out something big. I'm really just betting on them being able to figure something interesting out; the product and business always change."

In other words, he expected his investments to unfold in ways that he couldn't anticipate and in ways that the founders he invested in also couldn't anticipate. This sounded profound at the time, but I now regard it as blindingly obvious. I understand why he was annoyed at my question. If this weren't true, you'd have to believe that the founders weren't going to learn anything interesting after day one. Which is absurd.

This idea has massive implications for founders. Instead of planning in excruciating detail exactly what shape our business will take in year ten, we can simply embrace that *we can't know this right now—we'll figure it out over time as we obsess over finding PULL and serving customers.* When I embraced this for my startup, it was liberating. I stopped needing to pretend I could predict the future and instead was able to focus entirely on who had PULL right now. I stopped locking myself in that conference room in a futile attempt to craft the right plan. By just serving customers and paying attention to what their demand really was, our business unfolded into something I couldn't have predicted in advance; the things I tried to predict in advance would have certainly failed.

Just a few months after Offstream hit $100,000 in revenue, they hit $500,000 in revenue selling the exact same thing to the exact same market. While doing this, Varsha had a realization: One feature in Offstream's software product was desperately needed by many different kinds of green energy project developers. Because it was part of the company's software product, this was much more scalable than what they were currently selling. Did this represent a clear path to step 10, with $100 million in revenue? No. But it was an obvious step 2. And I have no doubt that as Varsha executes step 2, step 3 will unfold in a similar way.

"SCIENTIFIC" RESEARCH

Parker, the cofounder of a software startup called Jump, spent forty minutes walking me through a set of spreadsheets and slides to explain the fifteen months of research, experimentation, and validation work he and his cofounders had done. Parker was a Stanford MBA and a previous software executive. It showed: His team's thorough work seemed bulletproof. It was deeply logical and created a picture of a clear market need and opportunity.

And yet, he must have missed something, because his business wasn't getting traction. Prospective customers weren't buying, and he wasn't sure what to do. He felt stuck because all his research suggested that he had validated a massive problem and the perfect business opportunity. It all worked in theory, but something was off in practice.

This story is common. It is caused by ivory tower approaches to entrepreneurship that treat it like a research project. According to these theories, our job as an entrepreneur is to operate like a scientist: We do research, form hypotheses, run experiments, and validate our business before we build it. A cottage industry of consultants, speakers, and educators peddles this line of thinking. Like most academic theories, the scientific approach to startups is backed by rigorous logic. It sounds compelling, especially to highly educated founders. The only problem is that it simply doesn't work in the real world. Why?

As every founder learns in the pain cave, some percentage of our research doesn't translate to reality. This happens no matter how thoughtfully we approach our analysis, experimentation, and validation work. It doesn't matter how much time and effort we spend in the research stage, how many customer interviews we perform, or how excited people are about our idea and product. We're always missing answers to questions we didn't know we should have asked; we can't see the things we didn't know we should have looked for. In addition, we've almost certainly misinterpreted something we've heard from customers or seen in the data. Research errors send us to the pain cave; misplaced confidence in our research keeps us there.

Hard truth: Surveys, research, and even customer interviews that indicate that they *would be interested*—or even *would buy it in the future*—are worthless. Talk is cheap; actions show the truth. We only learn if demand is real when we try to sell something and see how buyers behave. This is the real path out of the pain cave. Use *sales,* then use *serving customers,* as real-world research.

As Parker and the Jump team learned the hard way, everything we learn *before* buyers consider paying money is worthless. This is, in part, because selling helps us separate what *is real* from what *seems real* in our research. But also, our prospective customers will only unveil their true PULL (to us *and* to themselves) when they are forced to get real and pay money.

To Parker's credit, he embraced this lesson. He started using sales as research, rather than a way to push his well-researched product, and had an uncomfortable sales conversation (covered in Chapter 5) that led to Jump's first customer. After that, Jump quickly grew from one to fifty customers in just ten weeks and to multiple million dollars in revenue in less than a year, becoming one of the fastest-growing early-stage startups in the United States.[1]

WHY I WROTE THIS

When I started my entrepreneurship journey, I guzzled a firehose of bad, complicated advice about entrepreneurship that all sounded right. This advice came from every direction: books, school, podcasts, social media. And it sent me straight to the pain cave.

It took me years in the pain cave to begin to figure out what actually matters. After building my first startup, I brought many struggling startups to—and beyond—their first million dollars in revenue. I have also seen many friends' companies die from a pattern of stupid, preventable, self-inflicted wounds. Along the way, I've been writing a weekly newsletter to make sense of it all. The topic has *pulled* me, and my newsletter subscribers have *pulled* this book out of me. This is the book I wish someone else had written and given me when I was just starting out to cut through the noise and focus me on what really matters. And while I am not a household name, haven't scaled a company to a billion dollars, and have yet to take one of my startups public, these things are step 10; PULL is step 1, and, after years of obsession, I feel like I finally understand it. I'm writing this book as much for my own startups as for yours and will happily spend my life toiling away building a deeper understanding of PULL—the most powerful force on Earth that's almost entirely ignored.

WHAT YOU'LL LEARN AND WHOM THIS IS FOR

The purpose of this book is to explore how new ventures become successful and escape the pain cave. It is not about building a commodity product, rolling up laundromats, cornering the avocado market, or side-hustling a passive income stream; it's about bringing something new into the world. In that sense, it's about *innovation,* not just entrepreneurship. My argument focuses on businesses where demand matters—where customers have the ability to make choices. This is most, but not all, startup ventures.

This book is mostly designed for entrepreneurs who have an idea or product and are trying to figure out how to turn their idea into reality, but it will also be helpful for entrepreneurs who haven't yet figured out their idea and those with a business that isn't growing as fast as they'd like. It is primarily about the early stage before startups take off (prior to, say, $1 million in revenue), but the concepts are applicable to companies at any stage that are looking to grow faster and stop pushing.

Importantly, this book is for entrepreneurs who play to win *and* not to lose, by working extremely hard over a long period of time. It is not for entrepreneurs who want some sort of overnight miracle. The latter is technically possible, but the playbook for that seems to be: Do what this book says, but get everything correct on day one. I wouldn't bet my life on that happening. Instead, I—and most founders—need an approach that doesn't feel like we're playing the lottery with our lives.

In this book, I've developed the simplest possible business framework (PULL) based on what works in practice. Critically, I've developed this based on observing how many thousands of individual buyers behave in sales and postsales conversations and how buyers' behaviors change at exactly the moment startups take off. From this foundation, I develop a practical model for innovation and company building.

This book's approach has been tested on hundreds of entrepreneurs across every continent. It has also been tested across industries, from exoskeletons to meal prep kits and software for chemical engineering plants.

The approach I teach in this book doesn't just help entrepreneurs build successful businesses. It also helps them do this faster, with less stress, distraction, and waste. Entrepreneurs stop feeling like there is an infinite number of things they *should* do and can focus on the few that actually matter.

To that end, what you'll learn in this book is also helpful for larger, established businesses who feel like they are misaligned, clunky, and stagnating. After all, if you don't understand how new businesses come to life, how can you possibly grow a business effectively and prevent it from becoming a calcified politburo?

In this book, we first explore the PULL framework. What exactly is PULL, and how does it work? When we find PULL, what do customers want to buy? What does a startup's path to PULL typically look like?

Then, we focus on tactics: How do we get PULL right? How do we sell and deliver? How do we "debug" our business when customers aren't pulling? How do we scale when customers *are* pulling?

Finally, we focus on PULL's many implications: Given PULL, what actually matters for building a fast-growing startup? And how do we stay sane while pursuing PULL and building our startup?

Ultimately, this book seeks progress. The only path to a bright future for humanity is through continued economic growth, and growth is only possible via innovation. Yet the current ivory tower approaches to entrepreneurship aren't just distractions; they prevent innovation. They hurt risk-takers and established businesses alike. They cause entrepreneurs to waste time on things that don't matter, making an already difficult task nearly impossible. They prevent would-be entrepreneurs from entering the ring because they have the wrong mental models about startups and are scared of getting started. More than anything, conventional business wisdom causes businesses to do everything *but* serve their customers—which prevents progress and hurts today's and tomorrow's society. I hope the simple ideas in this book will play a small part in the remedy.

PART I

PULL

CHAPTER 1

DEMAND

WHAT'S ON THE BUYER'S TO-DO LIST?

Fast-growing startups often seem to grow *despite* their best efforts.

HubSpot is a public software company with over a billion dollars in annual revenue. Prior to HubSpot, companies primarily found new customers by methods like cold calling and advertising. HubSpot was founded in 2006 on the insight that if businesses blogged online, their customers would come to them when searching for products and services on Google. If customers came "inbound" organically like this, it would save businesses money and frustration managing traditional "outbound" methods like cold calling. Yet at the time, all the blogging tools on the market were built for bloggers, not businesses. So HubSpot built a blogging tool for businesses to help them post content online that would get picked up by Google and show up in buyers' search results.

Here's the weird thing about HubSpot: For years, their product *barely* worked. Dharmesh Shah, the founder and chief technology officer at HubSpot, admits as much. "Every product I've ever launched was awful in the beginning," he says. Dharmesh is not exaggerating. HubSpot rebuilt nearly every piece of its product from scratch and turned over almost the entire product and engineering organization, just to get its product on the right track.[1] But here's the crazy part: This happened *after* the company's Series D financing round in 2011, when they were five years in, had $25 million in annual revenue, more than seven thousand happy customers,[2] and were the second-fastest-growing software-as-a-service startup in history.[3]

How is it possible that a company can grow that fast, *with happy customers*, seemingly *despite* their product?

Turns out, HubSpot's story isn't unique. When you get the inside story of almost every fast-growing startup, you hear something similar: The company is barely held together by duct tape and bubble gum, yet they seem unable to stop growing, no matter what they do! Mark Zuckerberg's description of Twitter is emblematic (and surprisingly common): "It's as if they drove a clown car into a gold mine and fell in."[4]

Most founders' experiences, however, are the exact opposite of this: No matter what we do, nobody seems to want our product or service. We thoughtfully design and build it, we hone our sales skills, we do tons of market research, we craft clever marketing, we get well-connected in the industry, we raise money from top-tier investors, we offer something that promises a compelling return on investment. And we mostly hear crickets.

Why did HubSpot grow fast (with happy customers) despite their product, while we grow slowly even if we seem to have it all together? Was it HubSpot's marketing hype, sales execution, value proposition, the "problem" they solved, lucky timing, or something else? Dharmesh explains: "It's easy to take an awful product in which there is strong interest and make it better through iteration. But it's really hard to take a great product in which there is little/no interest and generate interest. It's best to figure out [the] level of interest in the market as early as possible."[5]

So, in other words: HubSpot figured out what buyers wanted. Cool. This isn't helpful. It's no secret that the whole point of startups is to build something that people want. The legendary startup accelerator Y Combinator's motto is, "Make something people want." Why is this so difficult? What are we missing?

When we dig into the question What do people want?, things start to get interesting.

We're told that people want solutions to their problems and pain points. We're told people buy because of our compelling value proposition or unbeatable offer. Or worse: We're told that people want what we convince them they *should* want. Nope. These ideas are dangerous, because they *sound right* but lead us down a path of pushing something that nobody actually buys.

We need a precise way to think about what customers want, what they will *pull* out of our hands. We need, in other words, to understand *demand*. When Dharmesh at HubSpot talks about "the level of interest in the market," he's referring to demand.

If we don't find demand, we *push*, mostly unsuccessfully. If we do find demand, customers *pull*, and we grow effectively. If we find a *lot* of demand, we grow insanely fast. If we don't understand demand, nothing else makes sense or matters. So if we want to build businesses that work, we first need to deeply understand demand.

WHAT DO PEOPLE WANT?

In Economics 101, we were shown a graph about supply and demand: Demand represents people willing to buy supply. That made sense in the classroom, but when we're trying to bring something new into the world that people haven't seen yet, we need to understand demand at a deeper level.

So what *is* demand? In short: Demand is whatever buyers are trying to accomplish right now. Demand has been described as a "job to be done."[6] More concretely, we can envision demand as *the project a buyer is currently prioritizing on his to-do list*. When he has poor options for getting his project done, and we offer something that fits his project better, he buys it—pulls it out of our hands, really. In that situation, it's like our product is irresistible to him. It would be weird if he *didn't* buy it. On the other hand, when we sell something that doesn't fit the project he's currently prioritizing, or his current options are good enough, it would be weird if he *did* buy it. As a result, it feels like we're pushing.

This sounds simple. Obvious. You nod your head, say, "I already know this. Nothing new here."

I felt the same. I promise you, unless you've spent years hitting your head against the wall trying to grapple with the nature of demand, *you probably have it wrong*. I sure did.

Because demand seems obvious, the topic has not gotten the level of intense study it deserves. At best, demand is treated as step 18 in the 92-step entrepreneurial process: "After crafting a vision and writing a business plan, validate demand for your product." Sounds simple. Trite. Demand is therefore underestimated and misunderstood. Demand is not just another checklist item. Demand is the thing that *generates* our business; it pulls our product or service into existence. Nothing else we do matters if we don't find demand; find demand, and everything else mostly solves itself.

Most entrepreneurs get their first taste of real demand when something strange happens in their business. In a friend's case, after early customers required a ton of convincing, persuading, and flat-out begging before they would buy, one customer bought fast. My friend recalled receiving a phone call from a prospective customer she'd never met: "Hey, I heard about your product and found your phone number online. I need it right now. How do I sign up? Where do I pay?"

We typically hang up from a call like that and think, "Well, that was cool. I wish that happened more." And we get back to work, changing nothing. We chalk it up to customers being weird and unpredictable. Some buy fast; it's like they're pulling themselves through the process of buying and using our product or service. Others buy slowly; we have to push them, no, drag them kicking and screaming, through the exact same process. Nothing to be done about it. It's just how the world works.

This is a mistake.

If we understand demand, buyers' weird behaviors aren't so weird anymore. By understanding demand, we can find customers who *pull* and avoid wasting energy on those who need to be *pushed*. More than that, we can understand each customer's journey and predict what will cause them to move from push mode to pull mode—and what product they really need. When we design around buyers who pull, it takes less effort for us to grow. This translates to faster growth at lower costs and almost always leads to happier customers too.

Which sounds great in theory. But how do we do this? First, we need to unlearn two bad ideas that prevent us from finding demand.

UNLEARNING 1: DEMAND IS NOT DESIRE FOR A PRODUCT

Ryan Singer led strategy at a profitable software company called Basecamp. Basecamp has thousands of happy customers for their project management software and has been profitable for decades. If Basecamp was ever in the pain cave, it was back in the early 2000s, when I was still bleaching my hair.

Basecamp had what we founders might consider a *champagne problem*: Their thousands of happy customers would submit hundreds of feature requests. Ryan and the Basecamp team had to decide which of those requests to build and how to build them. As they spent years translating feature requests into features, they stumbled upon something fascinating: Even when customers told Basecamp exactly what feature they thought they needed, that didn't mean they *actually* wanted that feature. By digging into this contradiction, Ryan developed a foundational way to think about demand that helped me finally see it, after wasting years looking for demand where I'd never find it.

Here's the story:[7] Basecamp customers submitted feature requests for a permissions feature, where different users of the product management software aren't allowed to use particular features in Basecamp's product. When looking into the feature request, Ryan saw that customers had asked for the permissions feature to prevent people from being able to delete projects from Basecamp's project management application. This sounds like a reasonable request at face value: One person is able to delete the project for everybody, and we don't want that to happen.

Ryan started interviewing customers. He learned that on an important project, a contractor had completed her work and archived the project. She did this thinking she was archiving it only in her own view, but she had actually deleted the project for everybody. This caused the company that was working on the project, understandably, to freak out: Their important project had disappeared! As a result, the project manager wrote in to request a permissions feature. End scene.

Hearing this story, Ryan realized that demand *wasn't* for a permissions feature. Demand *was* for preventing team members from unknowingly archiving projects for everyone. Instead of spending months of engineering time building a complicated permissions feature, all Basecamp needed to build was a simple warning notification, triggered whenever someone clicked the button to archive a project, that said, "Are you sure? This will archive the project for everybody." Which would take a single engineer a few days. This simple warning notification wasn't just easier to build; it was also a better fit for what customers really needed than the permissions feature many had requested.

This story broke my brain. Previously, I'd thought demand meant "desire for a product." And so I would have looked at the permissions feature request and thought, "Clearly, this user has *demand for a permissions feature.*" But Ryan taught me that demand isn't about products or features at all. He saw that demand is something that exists *independently* of products or features. In other words, there is supply—our products, services, and features—and demand, which is *not* "desire for supply."

But if demand *isn't* "desire for supply," what *is* demand?

Demand is what buyers are trying to accomplish in their lives. Supply is what we build. These are two separate things. There is no such thing as demand *for* supply. *Demand exists as something independent, out there in the world, whether or not our supply exists, and whether or not we exist.* In other words, demand is supply agnostic.

The previous paragraph is the most important paragraph in this book. Get it tattooed somewhere. Everything else in this book, and in business generally, builds off of the idea that demand is *out there*—it exists in customers' lives, whether or not we exist. It is not "desire *for* a product" or about products at all.

Why is this so important? Because if we believe—as I always believed—that demand is *about* our products, or that demand is desire *for* our products, we can never find demand. We wind up looking in the wrong places: We think it's our job to "create" demand by making our product more desirable and persuading people they *should want it*. When we do these things, we are just pushing and polishing our supply; these activities have *nothing* to do with demand.

Why doesn't pushing our supply work? Because our supply doesn't create demand. It's the exact opposite: *Demand creates supply*. In Basecamp's example, the "permissions feature" request happened *after* the contractor archived a project for everyone. In HubSpot's case, "get customers to come inbound" was relevant *after* companies struggled to get customers via other methods. When people have demand, they look for supply that fits their demand, and they might buy something. Or they might hack together a DIY solution—literally *making their own supply for their demand*.

The idea that demand exists as an independent force that *creates* supply is both the most important thing to understand and the most difficult pill for entrepreneurs to swallow. There are four reasons why this is the case:

1. When people request features, it seems like there is *demand for that feature*. We've already covered this with the Basecamp story: When people request features, they are *requesting supply, not expressing demand*. We shouldn't take customers at their word when they request supply; we need to understand their demand and decide how to design supply that fits. Otherwise, we wind up wasting time building a bad-fit supply for their *real* demand.
2. When products fit demand really well, people behave as if they have demand *for* those products. It sure seems like people have demand *for* the iPhone, YouTube, Spotify, Louis Vuitton, you name it. People even get Harley Davidson tattoos! But remember the apple falling from the tree: It sure seems *as if* the apple wants to be on the ground, though that's not the case. Interestingly, the more it seems like people have demand *for* a product, the more useful it is to separate demand and supply. By doing this, we learn something very real about people's minds and what they're trying to do in their lives, which enables us to build things that people behave as if they really want.
3. All the lore about Steve Jobs and Henry Ford makes it seem like great entrepreneurs create demand, they don't find it *out there*. Don't they just envision a radically

different future and convince everyone to want that future? In short: When we find demand, it's up to us to design supply that fits. We may find demand that nobody else sees and, in response to this demand, design something that looks unlike anything that came before. Or we may find known demand and design supply that fits better than any other options on the market today. This is a less-magical way to understand how great entrepreneurs crafted successful innovations. On the other hand, designing supply that's innovative but doesn't fit anyone's demand simply can't work.

4. Accepting that demand is something we don't control requires a little humble pie. We founders live on the supply side and default to supply-side thinking. We love to focus on our products and services, our goals, our marketing and messaging and website. We want to believe that by making these better, we will succeed. We only succeed when we give up these supply-side fairy tales. This is humbling, especially for product-focused entrepreneurs. But it prevents being humbled by reality later.

Even when we embrace the idea that demand and supply are independent concepts, it is often difficult to tell whether someone—say, a potential customer—is talking about demand or supply. When customers talk about supply, they talk about things *we make and control*—things like features, functionality, and products. When customers talk about demand, they talk about things in their lives that *we don't control* and *aren't about supply*. Here's a handy guide:

Customer Expressing Demand	Customers Requesting Supply
I need to stop one person from archiving a project for everybody.	I need a permissions feature *or* I need to issue a mandate to my employees to stop archiving projects.
I need to manage our sales data.	I want a customer relationship management software tool.
I need to clean my kitchen.	I need a mop.
I need to think clearly again.	I need to see a mental health professional.
I need to look smart.	I need a copy of Rob's book.

UNLEARNING 2: DEMAND IS NOT ABOUT PROBLEMS

Well then, aren't we just looking for customers' problems and pain points? These are things that are happening in their world that aren't about our product, are they not?

No, no, no, no, *no*!

Parker, our Stanford MBA friend from the introduction, did an excruciating amount of research to figure out what people wanted. He showed me a spreadsheet where he meticulously analyzed more than one hundred prospective customer interviews. In each interview, he had asked his prospective customer to rank their problems and pain points on a one-to-ten scale, where ten was "most painful" and one was "least painful." This was his rigorous method to ensure his product was solving a real problem; in other words, to validate demand, that people wanted it. In his research, Parker found a pattern. One pain point was consistently ranked a nine or ten out of ten. Every interviewee could complain for hours about this pain point.

But then nobody bought Parker's product. And Parker realized that demand was something other than pain points.

Like Parker, we are taught a variety of reasonable ways to think about what demand might be: It's about their problems or pain points. It's about their desire for benefits or outcomes or value or ROI. These things *are* on the demand side, in that they are not necessarily about our product and its features. They sound right. When we look for them, we can typically find them.

But.

Someone can have serious pain points—and never *take action* to fix them. Life, in a way, is a series of pain points we mostly do nothing about.

Someone can have a big problem—and never *take action* to solve it. We have an impressive ability to cope with our problems.

Someone can want benefits, outcomes, value, ROI—and never *take action* to get them. Every business owner has a ton of high-ROI revenue-generating and cost-saving activities he won't ever prioritize.

And nobody is ever going to say, "You know what? You've described my pain points and problems and offered such compelling benefits . . . that I'm going to drop all my current plans and priorities to buy your product."

Pain points, problems, benefits, and the like all fail us because they don't effectively predict whether buyers will take action. Life gets much easier when we focus on *buyers' actions and their actions' causes*. Action, not problems or pain points, is the basis for demand. And we can understand buyers' actions (and therefore their demand) by focusing on what they are prioritizing on their to-do lists.

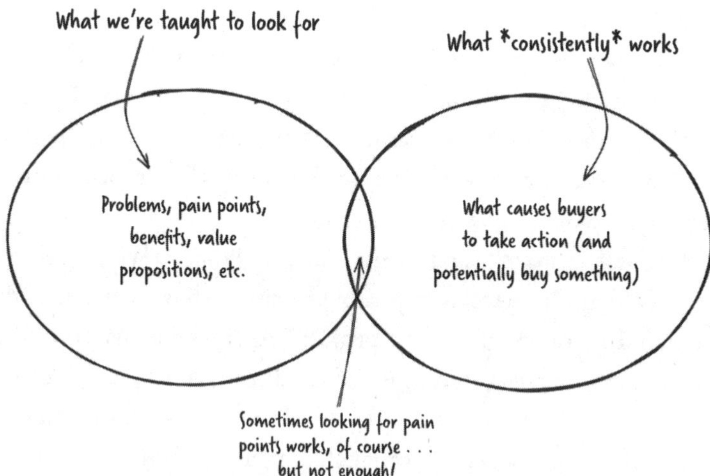

DEMAND IS ABOUT ACTION

Imagine that everybody has a to-do list in their mind that perfectly represents their priorities. In my mind, I envision a project management software screen, with categories of different things I want to get done:

Would be awesome to do this someday	Feels important but not sure how to do it	Have to do this, procrastinating	This is *the* priority right now

The to-do list in my brain is infinite. There are so many things I could theoretically do right now. But I'm human, so I can only focus on one thing at a time. Which means, out of my infinite list, I have to pick *one* priority right now.

I imagine a pitched battle going on in my head at all times as hundreds of plausible projects fight for my one priority slot. When I prioritize a particular project, it's not by accident—something *causes* one project to win over all the others. For example, when I got my first customer, a project immediately forced itself into my top priority: *How do I collect their payment?*

When a project is my top priority, I have *demand*. My demand is "to complete this project." And when this project is my top priority, it would be weird if I did anything else. In other words, you would have to push me—convince me, threaten me, force me—to do anything other than figuring out how to collect my first customer's payment. At any one point in time, for everything other than my current number-one priority, *I am not going to take any action*. I am in a "no-demand state" for an infinite number of other potential projects I *could* prioritize—which looks like this:[8]

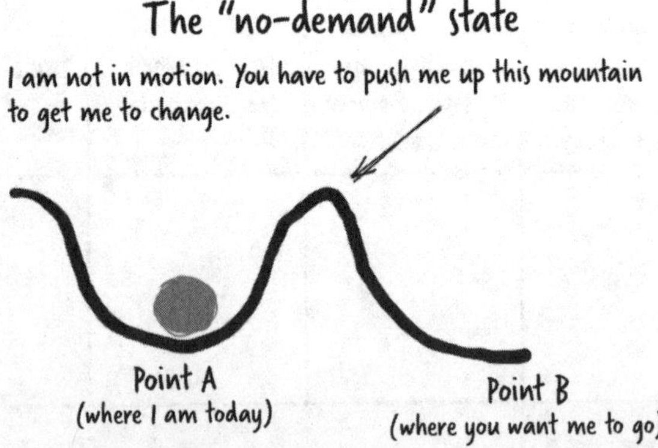

In this no-demand state, it's like there's a mountain between point A, where I am, and point B, where you might want me to go. I can complain endlessly about my problems and pain points at point A and talk about how nice it would be to be at point B, but am I really going to climb the mountain to get to point B? Probably not. "Bitchin' ain't switchin'," as Bob Moesta says. If you're going to get me from point A to point B, you have to push me up the mountain. When you do this, you are fighting gravity pushing me uphill, fighting against my no-demand state. And if you somehow manage to succeed in pushing me uphill, then you have to climb up the mountain again and again for every single customer. It's exhausting. This might work occasionally, but it's not easy to build a fast-growing business if we have to push a million people up a mountain.

Back to my to-do list. What *am* I prioritizing right now? The project: "Figure out how to collect payments from my first customer." Because I'm prioritizing this, it would be weird if I *didn't* take action on it. In other words, I am in a demand state for this project, which looks like this:

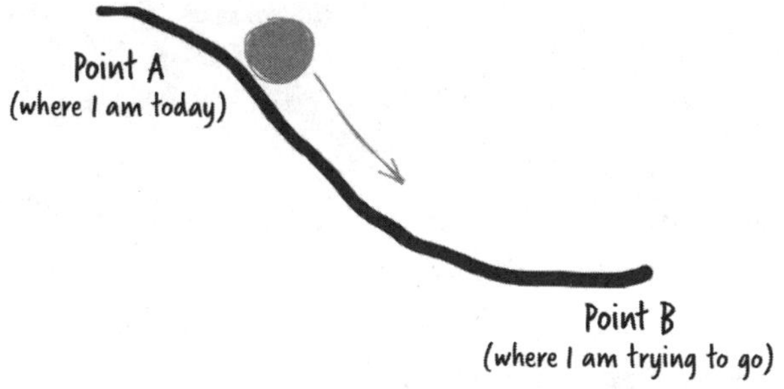

In this case, *not* taking action would be like defying gravity. If you have a tool that helps me get from point A to point B, you are working *with* my demand, not against it. In other words, you don't have to *push me* to point B, I might *pull you* to point B.

But just because I'm in this demand state, that doesn't mean I'll buy *your* product. When I'm in this demand state, I have to figure out exactly how to get from point A to point B. That's where supply fits in: Supply is *how* I get from point A to point B. Now, most people in a demand state can get from point A to point B just fine without you—whether they get there with a spreadsheet, a new hire, or their existing vendor. This means you are looking for someone in a demand state who has bad paths to point B—ideally they *can't* get to point B without you. When you find people in this situation, they would be weird *not* to buy your product.

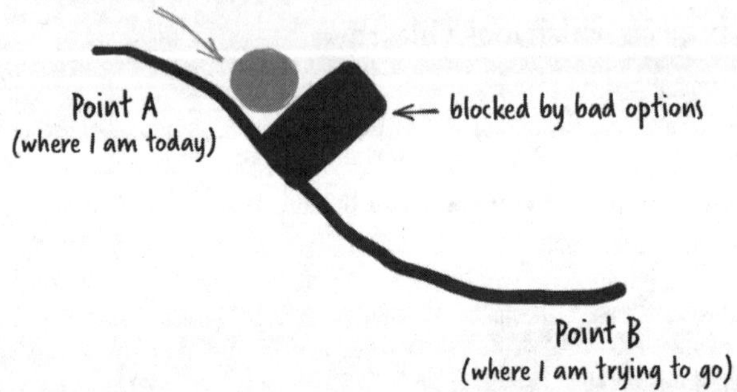

To summarize: When buyers are prioritizing a project right now but their existing options are unworkable—and you offer them something that unblocks them—they pull your product out of your hands; they behave as if it is irresistible.

Which is to say: It would be weird if people with demand and bad options *didn't* buy your product. Yet for everyone else (i.e., most people, most of the time), it would be weird if they *did* buy your product. The entrepreneur's job is to find demand and design around it; doing anything other than this is like trying to push a boulder up Mount Everest.

I've created a simple model that makes demand concrete so that you can apply this concept to your business right away.

Summary of the Mechanics of Demand
There is an infinite number of projects on my mental to-do list.
I can only prioritize one project at a time.
Something causes me to prioritize a particular project over all the others I could possibly prioritize.
When I prioritize a project, I have demand to get the project done. Everything else, I have no demand for.
As I prioritize a project, I consider different ways to get the project done. These are my supply options and include "do it myself" and "hire a person."
Most of the time, I perceive my options as good enough. When I have good-enough options, your startup is going to have a hard time getting me to buy, even though I have demand.
Sometimes, my options aren't good enough. They might not even be workable. In this case, if you offer me something that fits, I'll rip it out of your hands!

THE PULL FRAMEWORK FOR DEMAND

When would somebody be weird *not* to buy your product? When four things are true:

1. There is a *project* on their mental to-do list.

2. It is *unavoidable* right now (in other words, it's their number-one priority; they are in a situation where they can't not do it).
3. They consider a *list* of options for accomplishing this project.
4. But they think their options have serious *limitations* (ideally, they can't accomplish their project with the existing options—they are unworkable).

These four components create the PULL framework for demand.

P	U	L	L
A buyer has a **PROJECT** on their to-do list	that's **UNAVOIDABLE** right now.	They consider a **LIST** of options to get the project done	but they think their options have serious **LIMITATIONS**.
What is the buyer's ***PROJECT****?*	*Why is it* ***UNAVOIDABLE*** *now?*	*What* ***LIST*** *of options are they considering?*	*What serious* ***LIMITATIONS*** *do they think their options have?*

If you answer these four PULL questions, have you found PULL? Not quite! The difference between "we've arranged words nicely using the PULL framework" and "we've found PULL" comes down to a simple question: *Does it work?* More specifically: Do people exist who fit these four criteria, and if so, do they pull the product out of our hands?

We can think of this PULL framework, then, as a way to articulate a PULL *hypothesis*. This hypothesis is easily testable: We can (1) find people who *should* have these four characteristics, (2) see if they *do* have these characteristics, and then (3) see if they *pull*. This is the simple process by which startups find PULL; I cover this in more detail in Chapter 4.

Now, it's rare to find PULL on day one. More often, founders have to navigate their way from push to PULL. Two examples:

A friend was struggling, pushing his efficiency-improving tool toward HR executives. HR executives' efficiency project, like most projects in HR, was rarely unavoidable. Then he talked to outsourced HR providers, whose C-suite executives were all focused on efficiency because it made them more money and was core to their business. They had PULL and bought in days rather than months. This is a common evolution. Usually, a certain kind of person has PULL, while everybody else needs to be pushed. In this case, the entrepreneur succeeds by focusing only on those who have PULL—outsourced HR providers, not HR executives.

Another friend was struggling to sell his data migration tool to customer onboarding teams at software companies, until he realized that there wasn't PULL for "onboarding customers faster." Most people he spoke with weren't prioritizing speeding up their customer onboarding process, and in the rare case where they were, they had existing options they perceived to be *good enough*. He found there was PULL for "ripping and replacing your competitors' software products in no time"—enabling software companies to instantly migrate data from competitors' systems for a new customer who wanted to make the switch. There was PULL for "rip and replace," because software companies often lost a significant number of deals due to the perceived hassle of migrating from one tool to another, and there weren't good options for easily making the switch. In this case, my friend found PULL by simply reframing his understanding of his buyer's project, without changing the companies he was selling to or what his product did. The new framing connected with the project in buyers' minds; it was a project they constantly struggled with, to which they had barely workable existing approaches.

In both examples, the entrepreneurs found PULL over time. Critically, they knew their primary job was to find PULL, and they were self-aware when they were pushing—knowing that this was a signal that something needed to be fixed.

Even when we're looking for PULL, we often get stuck pushing something that makes logical sense, that we believe buyers should want. That phrase—*should want*—is enemy number 1 if we're trying to find PULL.

"SHOULD WANT" IS ENEMY NUMBER 1

As a kid, when I went to get my hair cut, I always felt vaguely dissatisfied with the result. If you had asked me why I felt dissatisfied, I wouldn't have been able to explain it. I had brought in a picture, say, of Matt Damon, and they had given me a haircut that looked like Matt Damon's haircut. So why was I unhappy?

Years later, I can finally explain it. I didn't want them to give me a haircut that looked like Matt Damon's haircut. I really wanted them to make me look like Matt Damon. That was the real project on my to-do list. Which is ridiculous. *Of course* Great Clips couldn't make me look like Matt Damon. They could cut my hair, but I was still going to look like, well, me.

By any logic, I shouldn't have wanted Great Clips to make me look like Matt Damon. My project made no logical sense. But that's the point: It doesn't matter what my project *should have been.* There's no law of physics that says I must be logical, or coherent, or even make decisions in my best interest. More bluntly: I am under no obligation to do things that make sense to you.

The same is true of our potential customers: What we think they should want, or how we think they should evaluate options, is irrelevant. They might not act in a way that maximizes shareholder value, or ROI, or units of utility. They act in a way that reflects whatever is happening in their brain. Ego, envy, and "how will others perceive me" can easily win out over straightforward ROI and functionality, because why wouldn't they? When we sit in our ivory towers and tell our potential customers what they should want, they may agree intellectually . . . and then they'll do something that doesn't make sense to us. Now, this doesn't discount the idea of projects and to-do lists; it just reinforces that we desperately need to understand what buyers' projects *really* are—because they are so rarely straightforward calculations of dollars and cents. Buyers' actions give us a hint of what's really on their mental to-do list.

Nearly every founder I've spoken with has gone through a period where they focused on what their customers, in the founder's opinion, *should* want. Projects that *should* be on their to-do lists. Things that are *good for them.* One entrepreneur told the story of trying to sell software to security engineers who, in theory, *should* want to find more security vulnerabilities at their companies. That's their job, right? His product promised to flag many more security vulnerabilities than their existing software tool would. It was hard to sell, and the founder couldn't understand why until a particularly honest security engineer told him, "There's no way I can buy this! It's going to make me look bad, like I haven't done my job in keeping our vulnerabilities low.

Plus, my bonus is based on having fewer vulnerabilities than last quarter. If I implement this, I lose my bonus!" The founder's logically sound pitch was the *exact opposite* of what was on the buyer's to-do list. It was *repulsive* to the buyer. You might think this is a rare occurrence, but I can assure you it is not.

Here's what's even harder to accept: *Your customers may not even be able to coherently articulate or explain a project on their to-do lists, even as they prioritize it.* People buy an endless number of self-help books and pay gobs of money to trained professionals to try to untangle what they *truly* want. It took me two decades to understand why I was dissatisfied with my haircuts, for example. I don't know if you could have interviewed me at the time and gotten me to admit it—to you *or* to myself. But here's what matters: If I had seen something promising I could "look like Matt Damon," I almost certainly would have acted on it. The same is true of our customers. It's often difficult for them to clearly articulate the thing they are *really* trying to achieve. This doesn't mean there's no demand, or that it's not worth trying to understand what they're trying to achieve. It simply means that we need to understand the to-do list in their brain based on observing *how they act.*

If "should want" is enemy number 1 that prevents startups from finding PULL, "will want" is enemy number 2.

"WILL WANT" IS ENEMY NUMBER 2

Ivan and Renan's startup MuukTest was born out of the founders' two decades of work experience in artificial intelligence (AI) and software quality assurance (QA). When software companies build new features in their products, the QA team tests those features to make sure they work properly before they are unleashed on customers. MuukTest had created a software tool that promised significantly faster and better testing than alternative QA software tools on the market. Instead of engineers manually coding hundreds or thousands of tests, MuukTest's product used AI and a point-and-click user interface to avoid almost all the manual coding work.

And . . . customers yawned. Ivan struggled to sell their software for just $200 per month per company. Their prospective customers took three or more months to evaluate the product. One in ten wound up purchasing after this long evaluation period, and the ones who did purchase required significant ongoing hand-holding from the MuukTest team to get *any* value out of the product. MuukTest's engineers almost always ended up doing the QA work for customers, and they used MuukTest's product to do so.

Three months of heroism to earn $200 contracts that require a lot of support is, to put it kindly, not good. MuukTest was stuck at under $10,000 in annual revenue, with a bank account balance quickly heading toward zero. Ivan asked for my help.

We started by reviewing Ivan's customer research. Their prospective customers, chief technology officers (CTOs) at growing software companies, explained how important QA was, how much quality mattered, and why they were doing their best to build high-quality software from day one. What they described seemed like a perfect fit for the product MuukTest had built. So why wasn't MuukTest's sales process working?

When we reviewed Ivan's sales calls, they told a different story. Most calls followed a similar pattern. CTOs would complain about their current QA practices. They didn't want customers to keep finding bugs. They needed to fix this. And yet, as they learned more about MuukTest, they got restless. Or their eyes glazed over. Something wasn't clicking, and it wasn't clear why. On one call, a frustrated CTO snapped, "I know I have to fix our QA, but I don't want to think about it. It should *just work*, so I can get back to building features that customers want."

Suddenly, it clicked. MuukTest was selling "the fastest AI-powered QA software on the market." This was based on what they had learned in their customer research. But their research, it seemed, had led them astray. In no-stakes interviews, buyers spoke confidently about what they would want in the future. And they weren't lying. Nor was MuukTest necessarily biasing their interview questions. Prospective customers just weren't revealing their true demand—to MuukTest or themselves—until the moment they grappled with taking action, when their project was unavoidable and they were forced to make a real purchasing decision. They were, in research calls, simply talking about the future—not expressing real demand.

When we ignored their research and *only* focused on what happened in the moment CTOs were considering buying something, the demand story became clear: CTOs were being forced to focus on QA because of a sequence of embarrassing software bugs. It was the CTOs' responsibility, but they didn't want to do it. CTOs' words and actions suggested that their demand *really* was, "Get QA off my plate and mind, so I can get back to doing what I really want to do: Building new features and managing my team."

By understanding demand, MuukTest's growth challenges made sense. *Of course* sales took months. Their buyers wanted to avoid thinking about QA, and MuukTest's product and sales process made them spend tons of time and effort thinking about

QA. *Of course* customers needed tons of support after purchasing. They wanted this to "just work," so they needed to be pushed to do anything!

At this point, Ivan had two options. He could fight against demand or embrace it. If he fought against demand, he would have tried to convince his prospective customers that QA is actually cool and important: They *should want* the MuukTest solution. But remember, *should want* is enemy number 1. This approach would almost certainly feel like pushing a boulder uphill. Ivan is brilliant, experienced, and persuasive, but even he would need a miracle to convince CTOs that the "necessary evil" of QA was actually something they wanted and needed.

On the other hand, if Ivan embraced demand, he would have to lean into the fact that, when buyers had PULL, their true project was something like: "Solve QA and keep it off my mind."

Ivan chose the practical route. Without changing their product one bit, he started selling MuukTest as "Quality as a Service." Using MuukTest's software, Ivan's team would set up and manage their customers' QA testing process for them. This was the exact same thing MuukTest's engineers were already doing for their customers. The only thing that changed was how customers perceived MuukTest; MuukTest now was a better fit for their PULL. The results were striking. Their sales conversations felt much better. Customers bought in three weeks, not three months. The crazy part? MuukTest was *forced* to raise prices: Their prospective customers were skeptical that a $200-per-month service could deliver the results they promised, and they expected to pay *thousands of dollars* per month for MuukTest. Despite paying ten or twenty times more, customers were happier postsale. As a result, MuukTest went from $10,000 in annual revenue to $1 million in annual revenue in under one year.

The implication? It doesn't matter what buyers say they *will want*. That's because demand only really takes shape when buyers have something at stake, *when they are actually prioritizing a project*.

In other words, *PULL is all about the situation, the "when."* When does a buyer need to take action? Why is their project unavoidable *at that moment*, not sooner or later? And *at that very moment*—at that when—what exactly is their PULL?

This teaches us a few critical things that help us find PULL:

1. The only trustworthy way to find PULL is by focusing on the moment when buyers are trying to take action.
2. Selling, as a result, is a highly underrated form of research.
3. We can't trust what we hear from people who haven't made a purchasing decision. We simply can't know (and neither can they) how and when their PULL will materialize. Whatever they express is likely to be enemy number 2, "will want."
4. Someone who has already made a decision may no longer have demand, but their experience can still be instructive. We can evaluate what their PULL was in that moment—because it was real.

PULL IS YOUR PATH OUT OF THE PAIN CAVE

What does PULL mean for you? You've probably been pushing your product on people who don't have demand. This is the default state: Every startup I speak with does this *because nobody gets taught about demand*. This means you're trying to sell to people who *should want your product* or *would benefit from it*, but you're running face-first into the reality that most people aren't prioritizing a relevant project on their to-do list. Or maybe, you've found people who have demand, but they perceive their options as "good enough." Even if you have a compelling value proposition, even if they have problems and pain points, even if you perfectly follow sales "best practices," even if they *say* they like your product and vision—it doesn't matter. You are playing on *hard mode*, if not *impossible mode*, when you try to push people who don't have PULL.

Which means you need to stop pushing and instead find PULL. This might require you to change something about your product, whom you sell it to, and/or how you describe it. Or maybe you're just starting out and can go out and find PULL *before* wasting years pushing a product the market won't pull.

Whether you're just starting out or have been hitting your head against the wall for years, you can find PULL.

The PULL framework should clear your mind too. When you understand PULL, you stop thinking in terms of problems, pain points, and desire for your product. You stop thinking about what buyers *should want* or believing them when they describe what they *will want*. You clear out all that clutter and simply focus on what your potential customers are trying to accomplish right now. And you finally understand a few important things.

- **Why a lot of your research hasn't translated to revenue:** Your research almost certainly surfaced tons of interesting information about problems and pain points. But because your customer research didn't uncover your customers' PULL, you almost certainly learned things that were red herrings; they felt right but didn't translate to revenue or the right product or service.

- **Why some people buy fast and others buy slow:** It's about what was happening in the customers' world, on their to-do list. It's not a coincidence or luck: They had prioritized a project that your product or service fit. Every startup's sales cycle is just the sum of (1) time until the customer prioritizes the project on their to-do list, plus (2) a few minutes, days, or weeks (however long it takes for them to actually purchase your product once they decide to buy it). When you don't understand demand, it just seems unpredictable.
- **How to grow:** Instead of trying to convince a bunch of people to buy your product, your core growth activity is to find people who have PULL. Assume that you can't convince anyone of anything. In other words, the primary task of growing a startup is finding the people who need no convincing.
- **Why your conversion rates are low:** You should focus your business—your messaging, how you design your product or service, how you price—on people who have PULL, not people you're trying to convince that they *should* prioritize the project, or people with good-enough options. When we design our business around people whom we're trying to convince, we wind up overbuilding and underpricing for people who simply won't value what we're doing—no matter how hard we push.

The path out of the pain cave, then, is simple: Stop pushing your product onto people who would be weird to buy. Find PULL, and you'll know exactly who would be weird *not* to buy.

ZOOMING OUT

When we understand demand, we can finally answer the simple question at the core of startups: Why do fast-growing companies grow fast? In short, because each buyer *pulls*, and there are a lot of buyers who have PULL at the same time.

Let's return to HubSpot as a simplified example. In their case, B2B companies were always focused on "getting new customers," but HubSpot offered a modified project: "Get new customers *to come to you online, without cold calling*." This was a better shape of the *real* project on the mental to-do list of a buyer who, for example, was struggling to make cold calling work and wanted an easier way to get customers. Because cold calling is quite difficult to do and manage, this buyer has a project that not only is unavoidable with bad options but also is *constantly* on their to-do list. When someone in this situation heard about HubSpot, they *pulled*.

Even if HubSpot's project *only* replicated with companies that were struggling to make cold calling work, *almost every company that does cold calling struggles with it almost all the time*. Which meant that, for HubSpot, basically everyone they could sell to had PULL all the time.

This means a company's current market size is situational (based on who currently has PULL), not simply demographic (based on who people are). In other words, market size is based on *when* people are prioritizing a specific project, not just *who* could theoretically prioritize that project. Fast-growing companies have found a single unavoidable project for a lot of buyers right now, with comparatively bad supply options.

This model also gives us a practical place to find demand: By observing our potential buyers' situations and actions, we can reverse-engineer the projects they had and options they faced to understand their PULL. This is a more sensible, less error-prone form of research than how entrepreneurs typically approach customer interviews, where we *think* we're looking for "desire for our product" or "pain points" and wind up seeing demand where there is none. Instead, we grapple with what they're doing in the real world (i.e., by observing them or doing their job with them) and use that as a ground truth to form the to-do list in their mind. When we model our buyers' to-do lists based on their real actions, we find a place where we can fit. As we will see in the coming chapters, we can craft our PULL hypothesis, show it to prospective customers, and observe how they act in response to our PULL hypothesis. When we get this right, it's weird if they *don't* buy our product or service. With the PULL model, observing customers turns into fascinating detective work rather than the existential and futile "how do I convince them to want my product" stress.

The PULL framework is designed around the individual buyer. But we can use it to zoom out and see waves of demand across industries that predict how new products diffuse in the market. When a new regulation is introduced, a project is prioritized at every company: *Figure out how to comply with the regulation.* Unlike regulation, which hits everyone all at once, demand waves usually break across the economy unevenly. As companies use AI to accomplish business goals, they run into challenges that force projects onto their priority lists, like: How do we avoid AI hallucinations? Because companies adopt AI at different paces, this project is unavoidable for different companies at different times. But beware when zooming out: Many startups focus on broad trends, like AI, but never zoom in to find a single buyer's real PULL. As a result, they create some fancy product or service and try to convince buyers they *should want it* (and usually, nobody does). Startups only succeed if they find PULL, and PULL only exists on the to-do lists of individual buyers.

I often hear the questions: Are all the best company ideas behind us? or When artificial superintelligence arrives, will there be any more businesses to build? As long as humans have to-do lists in their brains, demand will be never-ending, and opportunities for innovation will always exist. Unlike the utopian thinkers who believe that once everybody has some amount of material wealth we'll have no more needs, I'm quite confident we're wired to have never-ending to-do lists in our brains. Each completed project creates the space for more projects. Our brains aren't wired to be able to handle empty to-do lists. Demand is human.

More practically, if our goal is to build a company that doesn't die and has the chance to grow fast, we need to find PULL and design around demand, versus getting stuck pushing our product from the supply side. The supply side is so seductive: It's what we control and what we want to focus on. Most entrepreneurs, me especially, want to live in the fantasy world where we get to design our products and services, and the world just "gets it" and showers money and adoration upon our brilliance. Only when we kill the supply-side fantasy and embrace the hard truth that, by default, nobody wants our product or cares what we think they *should* want, do we have the chance to find demand in the real world and, in response, design our supply as a better-fit option.

Demand is what buyers are trying to achieve. It is the project they are prioritizing on their to-do list right now. We don't control their priorities or the options they consider, and none of this has anything to do with our product. When we understand their project, when they prioritize it, which options they consider, and why they think these options aren't good enough, we don't just know whom to sell to. We know exactly what they will PULL—and from this, we can derive everything else about our business.

CHAPTER 2

SUPPLY

WHAT FITS THE BUYER'S DEMAND?

The potential customer, a director at a nonprofit, vented: "Since I've been at this organization—three years now—our existing software tool has been really frustrating. It's not made for our industry, it's hard to use, we've spent a bunch of money on consultants to improve it, and we've still struggled to use it to manage our career and internship programs. About a year and a half ago, my boss told me to start looking into alternatives. Now that we're going out to get new funding, our current system just isn't representing our impact—metrics like attendance, completion rate, and outcomes—in reporting to funders."

Sruti, the founder of a software startup called Campground, listened as the potential customer explained his problems and pain points in detail. Sruti had started Campground for this exact reason: Existing software tools were not designed for nonprofits that were trying to manage their career and internship programs. Campground was an all-in-one tool for them to manage these kinds of programs.

So it seemed like Campground was a perfect fit for what this potential customer needed.

Or was it?

The first red flag: As the call continued, Sruti learned that despite the nonprofit's current system being frustrating for three years, and despite being told to look into alternatives over a year ago, *this was the prospective customer's first attempt at looking into his options.* Did he really have demand?

The second red flag: Sruti had spoken with hundreds of nonprofit directors just like this one. And the same thing always seemed to happen: They would have a great conversation. The potential customer would say, "Wow, this is amazing. We really need this. You really understand us." And then? They would very rarely buy Campground's product, even if Sruti offered discounts, sent follow-up emails every week for months on end, and followed all the sales best practices she'd been taught.

As a result, Sruti constantly felt like she was pushing her product onto people who didn't want to buy it. She felt this way despite her potential customers saying they wanted it, needed it even. Despite Sruti's pitch deeply resonating. Despite Campground's product being clearly valuable—Campground's existing customers gave raving testimonials. Something was off, and it seemed to come down to these good calls that didn't lead to purchases.

We don't have to look far for the answer—it's hidden in plain sight, in the buyer's quote. But without the PULL framework, the buyer's monologue is a tangled mess, what I call a "demand hairball." Using the PULL framework, we can untangle this hairball and tease out what demand might be: Hmm . . . this prospective customer has coped for three years without doing anything, so he could theoretically cope for thirty. His default seems to be "cope with our current systems." Why not continue to do that? Why is that default option no longer workable?

Because we now know what to look for, we can see the hint in the buyer's quote. Why is he starting to talk to vendors now? In our words: What's changed in his situation that's causing him to (potentially) have an unavoidable project where his current options might not cut it anymore?

Ah, there it is: This buyer is finally talking to vendors because his nonprofit is trying to raise money, and his current approach isn't cutting it reporting-wise. From this, we can reverse-engineer his project: *Fix my reporting so fundraising is easier.*

Before Sruti understood this, she described Campground as an all-in-one tool for nonprofits to manage their career and internship programs. Sruti would explain how difficult it is for nonprofits to manage their programs, often cobbling together a bunch of different software tools—for example, one tool to manage event attendance, another to administer course materials, another to coordinate volunteers, another to communicate with program participants. Campground brought together all the nonprofits' different tools into one centralized system, which therefore made their programs easier to manage.

Sruti's description was thoughtful and logical. Prospective customers even agreed with her assessment of how difficult it was to manage nonprofit programs across different tools. She had pleasant sales calls, where they said nice things, like, "You totally understand us! This is so relatable. Everything is scattered across different tools. We totally should have an all-in-one tool!"

And then they didn't buy. It was a coin flip as to whether they'd buy after a year of Sruti persistently following up with them.

Here's why this happened. Campground, as Sruti described it, was a good fit for fixing nonprofits' clunky and scattered systems. This was what buyers complained about—but could keep complaining about for years without doing anything. It wasn't real demand. It wasn't their real project. Unfortunately, Campground's pitch was a *terrible* fit for the nonprofit's project; what they actually needed to change was their reporting: Fix my reporting so fundraising is easier. Because Sruti misunderstood demand, her pitch made buyers *less* likely to buy. Sruti thought that buyers would be thrilled to no longer have to cobble together different systems. Instead, buyers heard about Campground and got overwhelmed with how much effort it would be for them to switch everything over to a new system. Even though Sruti's pitch resonated with buyers intellectually, it actually created a new, scary project in their minds: "Go through a painful migration of all our existing program management tools." Even worse: Based on Sruti's pitch, it wasn't even clear prospective customers would get the better reporting they needed! Sruti and her prospective customers were speaking different languages because Sruti misunderstood their PULL.

So Sruti faced a choice: Figure out how to sell something that fit buyers' demand or continue to push and suffer through infuriatingly long sales cycles and low conversion rates. It wasn't a difficult choice.

Sruti started by articulating her buyers' *real* project. Then she understood what options these buyers were looking into for their "fix reporting" project, and why buyers thought their existing options weren't ideal. Turns out, they were considering hiring a data analyst to do reporting or getting a consultant to create reports and dashboards for them, but they worried these options would be expensive and slow.

P	U	L	L
What is the buyer's ***PROJECT****?*	*Why is it* ***UNAVOIDABLE*** *now?*	*What* ***LIST*** *of options are they considering?*	*What serious* ***LIMITATIONS*** *do they think their options have?*
Fix reporting so fundraising is easier.	We are struggling to fundraise because our data is scattered and we can't explain our impact.	• Hire a data analyst. • Get a consultant.	They are too expensive and slow.

Given this, what will buyers pull? Given their demand, what should Sruti's supply be?

To answer this, Sruti asked herself the supply question: *What can we offer buyers that fits their PULL better than their alternatives?*

When we understand PULL, the answer to this question is pretty obvious. Here was Sruti's one-sentence answer: Campground offers a donor reporting solution that gets customers funder-ready reporting faster and more affordably than consultants or hiring data analysts, plugs into their existing systems, and requires little work from them to set up or use.

See what happened there? Sruti described Campground in a way that made sense to buyers in the context of their demand.

You can guess what happened next: Buyers stopped zoning out and started leaning in. She heard things like, "If you can really do this, I'll give you all my money." Talk is cheap; the real testament came a few weeks later. Sruti sent me a message: "I'm SHOCKED. We just converted a $25k deal in less than a month turnaround time (⅓ our usual) and 5x our usual deal value."

This shouldn't be shocking. It's what happens when we find demand and describe supply in a way that fits demand, rather than describing (and pushing) a product that doesn't obviously fit buyers' demand.

And here's the amazing part. Sruti didn't have to change Campground's product at all to use this supply description in her sales calls: Her product already had the reporting capabilities buyers wanted. She simply stopped describing her product the wrong way. In addition, this made Campground's product and business direction much clearer. Instead of having a variety of different features on their product roadmap that made prioritizing difficult, Sruti knew exactly which features would actually move the needle: More reporting features!

But here's the interesting thing: When we look at Campground's description of demand and supply before and after this change, both articulations make sense (see table on the next page).

Both supply descriptions look reasonable and logical. The former is what Sruti thought buyers should want, but it didn't reflect their PULL at all. They just wanted better reporting, and Sruti was offering something that wasn't obviously going to improve their reporting and was going to require them to do a lot of work switching out all their systems, and for what? Better-running

PULL	Before: Program Management	After: Reporting
What is their **PROJECT?**	Make our programs easier to run.	Fix reporting so fundraising is easier.
Why is it **UNAVOIDABLE** now?	We've struggled with our existing systems for years.	We are struggling to fundraise because our data is scattered and we can't explain our impact.
What's on their **LIST** of options they consider?	Continue to use our existing systems.	• Hire a data person. • Get a consultant.
What serious **LIMITATIONS** do they think their options have?	They are clunky and annoying.	They are too expensive and slow.
What is our **SUPPLY**?	A program management tool that makes their programs much easier to run in one all-in-one, fit-for-purpose system that's a comparable price to their existing systems.	A donor reporting tool that gets them funder-ready reporting faster and more affordably than consultants or hiring data analysts, that plugs into their existing systems, and that requires little work from them to set up or use.

programs? Sure, that would be nice—but that wasn't what they were prioritizing right now. In their minds, they would still have to fix their reporting for funders after implementing Campground. As a result, Sruti was in push mode. The second supply option reflects and fits buyers' PULL much better than the first one, and Sruti felt the difference viscerally in her sales calls.

Let's dig into the idea of supply, so we can craft supply that buyers pull.

WHAT IS SUPPLY?

I've worked with startups building mind-bending new technologies out of Harvard and MIT research labs. Their path is always the same:

1. Do something crazy in a lab.
2. Try to figure out how to commercialize it.

Just about every founder follows a similar path, even if we don't get to nerd out in a research lab. We almost always start with a *product idea,* rather than PULL. Usually our product idea comes in the form of: Wouldn't it be cool if we built X? or Isn't there a big market opportunity for Y? In other words, we begin with the product or service we think *should exist.*

Eventually, we try to describe our idea to potential customers. And we realize there is an infinite number of potential descriptions, value propositions, and sales pitches that could work for our product idea. Most startups die here when all of these things that could work in theory don't work in practice. If we succeed, it's because we stumble across demand. And if we are lucky enough to find demand, we usually then look at our product or service idea and realize it's a square peg to demand's round hole.

It doesn't matter how grand our startup idea is, how magical our technology is, why we're unique and special, or how exactly our product or service works: If it doesn't *fit* someone's PULL, it's extremely difficult to get anyone to buy it. When we understand demand, our task is to shape our product or service into supply that is a good fit for the buyer's demand.

How should we think about supply? *If demand is a buyer's project, we can think of supply simply as the project plan we propose to get it done.*

The PULL framework tells us what supply will fit: Buyers are trying to accomplish X project, but their existing options are unworkable because of Y. When this is the case, our supply just needs to help buyers *accomplish X project without Y.* When we describe our supply this way, buyers with PULL get it and pull.

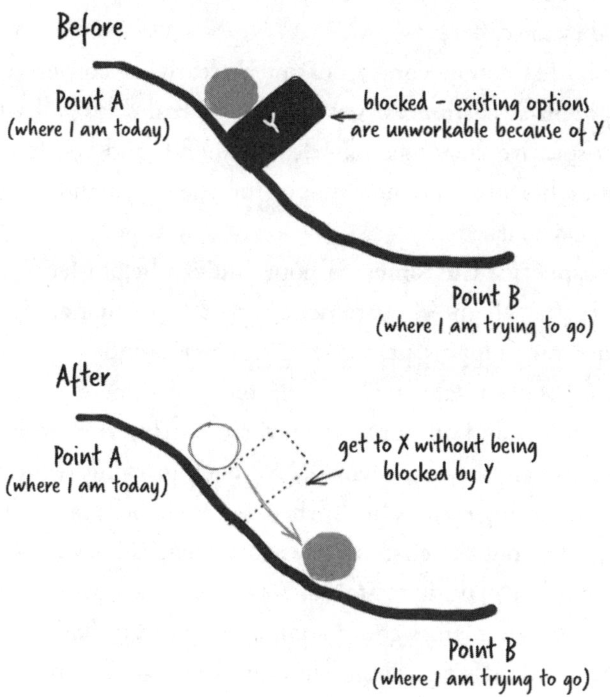

The bad news is that this simple exercise is counterintuitive to our brains as founders. We think we're supposed to describe our ingenious product, vision, and on and on. This feels right:

They're buying the product, aren't they? Don't they need to see it in all its glory and understand all its bells and whistles? But this approach, as you've probably experienced, doesn't work very well.

SUPPLY VERSUS PRODUCT (OR SERVICE)

The mind-bending activity is to separate two things that seem like they should be synonyms: *supply* versus *our product (or service)*. They are different.

This distinction comes out most clearly in conversations with potential customers. Let's look at a real sales call where the prospective customer has clear demand, and the founder describes his product, not supply for their demand. It goes poorly, as you'll see.[1]

Prospective Customer: "I hope you can help! Here's some context: We sell an AI customer support agent that acts like a real customer support person. E-commerce brands buy our AI customer support agent to handle *their* customers' questions at peak hours and off hours when their existing customer support team can't handle them. We've been growing really fast, but we are a tiny team. One of the biggest challenges we face is making sure our AI customer support agent is answering correctly and not making mistakes. As we've grown, we've started to get some complaints about quality. We need to find a way to solve this, because right now I'm only sleeping a few hours per night because I have to read through every conversation transcript myself. I can't find any solution out there, and I've been searching."

Based on what this prospective customer is saying, here's her PULL:

P	U	L	L
What is the buyer's ***PROJECT****?*	*Why is it* ***UNAVOIDABLE*** *now?*	*What* ***LIST*** *of options are they considering?*	*What serious* ***LIMITATIONS*** *do they think their options have?*
Identify low-quality conversations so we can fix our AI agent, without all the manual work we're currently doing.	Losing sleep doing all this manual work.	Continue doing manual work; looked for other solutions but couldn't find anything.	There isn't an automated solution.

At this point, the founder should explain his *supply*: How his startup's product fits this PULL. In other words, how would he help this prospective customer identify low-quality support conversations? This could be done simply, in one minute or less, by saying, "That's exactly what we help with. We plug into your AI system and automatically flag any low-quality conversations to you for further review. You can get notified by email or chat. Is that directionally what you're looking for?"

Instead, the founder thinks he needs to explain his product and the problem it solves. Here's what that looks like:

Founder: "Thanks for sharing that. I think we might be a good fit for you. Let's start with our thesis on the problem. We call it the AI observability problem, and it's massive. We estimate it costs companies $55 billion a year and will only get worse over time. Here's the root cause: If we look into the nature of AI . . . [The founder continues explaining AI observability for three minutes.]"

At this point, the founder shares slides that walk through the AI observability problem, its market size, and why it's such a big problem. The prospective customer nods and might even find this informative. But in the back of their mind, they're thinking, *Can you actually help me accomplish my project?*

Founder: "Now, let me show you a high-level overview of what we're building: the future of voice observability! Our vision is to make building AI agents seamless with a web and mobile application that makes sure worrying about quality is a thing of the past . . . [The description continues for three minutes.]"

Here, the founder shares a picture of a fancy-looking software product. This picture makes the buyer think the startup offers a fancy-looking software tool, *whether or not she needs a fancy-looking software tool.* More importantly, the buyer starts to get overwhelmed with how much there is to learn. She still isn't sure whether this will help her accomplish her project at all.

Founder: "Let me walk through how exactly it works. Basically, there are four different parts of the product. Our ingestion engine allows us to import all of your conversation transcripts, while our evaluation engine then finds . . . [The description continues for four minutes.]"

The founder displays a diagram of how their product works—how its different modules fit together. By now, the prospective customer is overwhelmed and confused. This seems complicated, and she still has no idea what pieces of it are relevant to her project and which aren't. A lot of words, concepts, and visuals are getting thrown at her. She doesn't even know the right questions to ask to figure out if this will help her. Maybe it will make sense to her if she asks about someone else who is using this?

Prospective Customer: "Who is currently using this? Can you give me an example of a company that's using this for their AI agent?"

Founder: "Ah, so the product is still in development, but we are signing on design partners . . ."

A faraway look appears in the prospective customer's eyes; she wasn't going to get relief or sleep. She couldn't understand what this founder was trying to pitch her, what product the founder could actually deliver, and whether it would help her accomplish her project. It seemed like both overkill and underkill: overkill, in that there were so many moving pieces to this pitch and solution that seemed irrelevant to her project; underkill, in that it wasn't clear that anything had been built yet that would actually help her sleep at night.

The call ended, and the prospective customer never emailed the founder back. The founder was confused because he felt like the call went well. She had asked thoughtful questions and seemed to have demand. Had he not conveyed enough urgency?

In this case, the customer should have bought but didn't. Unfortunately, this is not atypical. If you've tried to sell something to customers and felt like they didn't "get it," it was almost certainly because you were describing your product (or service)—not *supply for their demand*. Even if they had real demand, you guaranteed they wouldn't buy from you.

Product vs. Supply	Our Product	Supply for Their Demand
What we describe	From our perspective, how does the product or service work? What are its components?	From our customers' perspective, how do we help them accomplish their project better than their alternatives?
What happens	Prospective customers are confused.	Prospective customers get it.

The difference between supply and product is most visible in one-to-one sales conversations because the feedback is visceral:

We look into buyers' eyes as they get confused and annoyed. Their rejection is unignorable and personal. We see it and feel it.

But this problem isn't just in sales calls. It's on our websites, in our advertisements, really *everywhere*: Most of the time, when potential customers ask a startup founder, "So how can you help? What does your company do?" they need to pull up a chair and pull out a dictionary (and perhaps a rosary) to get through the answer.

Conflating *supply* and *product* leads to all sorts of pain for startups. We often interpret customers' confusion as a reason to spend more time on product development and build more features. The previous founder spent months and hundreds of thousands of dollars overbuilding a complicated product, when he could have built something simple in a few days that would have been a good-enough fit for the buyer's demand.

Or we interpret customer confusion as a sign that we should pivot our business because it isn't working. Or that we should *push harder*. None of this works.

Product versus supply highlights a disconnect between what's in our minds and what's in our prospective customers' minds. This explains the famous Peter Drucker quote: "The customer rarely buys what the company thinks it sells him."[2] We think we're selling our product. Customers are buying supply for their demand. Misunderstand this subtle difference, and even if you find PULL, buyers won't buy because they can't figure out what you're selling.

DESIGNING GOOD-FIT SUPPLY

Demand and supply operate by different physics. We find demand—PULL—*out there* in the world; we *design* supply to fit demand better than their existing options.

Contrasting Demand and Supply	
Demand	**Supply**
The project on their to-do list.	Our project plan to accomplish their project.
We find demand.	We design supply.
Upstream of supply; causes supply to be relevant (or not).	Downstream of demand.
We don't control demand.	We control supply.
PULL exposes a gap.	Supply fills the gap.

Assuming we've found PULL, defining our supply is relatively straightforward. We simply answer the supply question: What can we offer buyers that fits their PULL better than their alternatives? This takes all of two minutes.

This question sets the bounds—or requirements—for the product or service we offer. Once we know PULL's requirements, it's up to us to design a solution that fits. Sometimes, this requires us to invent new things. Other times, we simply combine existing technologies, materials, inputs, and so on in some new pattern that fits demand. Whether we need to invent something new or combine existing options depends on what PULL demands.

Whatever supply we offer, if it meets two criteria, a buyer will pull.

Criterion 1: Do Buyers Get It?

When we describe our supply, buyers should get it. Fast. Buyers typically need to answer these four simple questions:

1. What is it?
2. How is it different from my other options?
3. How does it help me accomplish my project? (Or, more simply, how does it work?)
4. What does it cost?

Interestingly, more description isn't necessarily better—in fact, it is often worse. The more words, visuals, and concepts we add, the more likely we are to confuse them with things that aren't relevant to their demand. I often joke that each extra thought a buyer needs to process reduces their likelihood of buying by 25 percent. Except, it's not really a joke.

Each startup's supply description evolves over time through conversations with customers. We learn what questions they *actually* ask when they have PULL and refine our supply description accordingly so that it fits with no unnecessary thinking required.

Criterion 2: Does It Fit Their True PULL?

Sometimes, a buyer has PULL, understands our supply, and chooses a different (often inferior) option. This is infuriating. Here's why it happens to Sruti at Campground, and why it happens to you and me as well.

Campground is faster and cheaper than a nonprofit's other options. So buyers will always choose Campground, right? Not so fast! Even though Campground is better than alternatives along the dimensions of speed and cost, buyers might decide, as they approach their purchasing decision, that their real PULL is different: "Yes, a consultant is more expensive and slower, but what we've decided really matters is getting an expert's guidance."

In this case, a buyer is satisfied *because* they spent ten times as much as they would have on Campground on a grizzled non-profit consultant. If this happens frequently, it could lead to Campground adding an "expert-on-call" to their supply.

Our job is to understand buyers' PULL and describe supply that fits. Even if we understand this, it's not a guarantee that every single buyer will buy. But if we do this right, it would be weird if the ones who have PULL that we uniquely fit *didn't* buy.

DEMAND AND SUPPLY ANSWER (JUST ABOUT) EVERY QUESTION YOU HAVE

Without the concepts of demand and supply—and specifically the PULL framework—we always seem to wind up using a million artifacts and methodologies to describe, define, price, and differentiate our product: roadmaps, positioning statements, messaging, taglines, features and benefits, to name a very small subset. These artifacts take months to create, and we wind up with a stack of documents that all seem individually important but aren't collectively coherent and that nobody at our startups actually understands. Then, any time we learn something new, all these artifacts need to be updated, and our business needs to be reinterpreted. This is a headache and slows us down. If, on the other hand, we simply use the concepts of demand and supply, we may never need much else.

Here's how to use the concepts of demand and supply to answer some of the most challenging questions we face.

How Do We Price Our Product?

Entrepreneurs often struggle to answer questions like: How do I price my product? This is the kind of question that is impossible to answer without first understanding demand and supply, yet intuitive and obvious once we do understand demand and supply.

Using Campground's example, how should they price their product? The most money Campground could possibly charge is based on how much completing the project is worth to the buyer: Fix my reporting so fundraising gets easier. What is this worth to the nonprofit? How much money does the nonprofit think they could raise if they had better reporting? Say the nonprofit CEO believes they could raise another $1 million per year if they had better donor reporting. If Campground charged $1.1 million per year, it would be weird if the nonprofit bought their product. But if they charged $900,000, would the nonprofit buy?

Well, no. While the value of the project dictates the maximum the buyer would theoretically pay, remember: The buyer considers different options, like hiring someone whose sole job is donor reporting or bringing in a consultant. A consultant might only charge $50,000. A new hire might cost $100,000. So as Sruti thinks through how to price Campground, she has to triangulate across the value of the project and the costs of the alternatives. When Sruti first sold Campground as a program management tool, she charged around $5,000 per year for it and decisions took months. When Sruti sold Campground as a reporting tool, she charged over $25,000 per year for it, and decisions took weeks. This sounds crazy until we understand the mechanics of demand and supply, and then it seems obvious.

What Is Minimum Viable?

Here's a question that has sent entrepreneurs to the pain cave for decades: What do I need to build and deliver for the first version of my product or service?

When I finally started getting traction for my first company, customers wanted to buy something very different than what our team had built. We had built a software tool for employee scheduling. Customers wanted an employee recruiting tool. We didn't have the time to build an employee recruiting tool, so I *became* the employee recruiting tool. I did everything customers needed in a hodgepodge of spreadsheets, text messages, and emails.

Customers couldn't log into the recruiting software they had purchased because, well, it was a spreadsheet—there was no software tool to log onto! Instead, they received emails from me about new candidates and their recruiting status. I apologized to potential customers, promising that they'd be able to log into a software tool in a few months. One customer replied, "Honestly, I like this better because it just works in my email, and I don't have to learn some new tool." I stopped apologizing for not having a customer log-in. In a weird twist, "You don't have to learn a new tool" became one of the big selling points for our recruiting solution. This janky-seeming supply fit my customers' demand better than a fancy online portal and interface would have.

The book *The Lean Startup* created the brilliant concept of a minimum viable product (MVP). The idea is that we should avoid overbuilding things that customers might not want and instead build as little as humanly possible. We should go out and test our MVP in the world with customers ASAP. If it doesn't work, then we should pivot and try something else.

There's a simple reason this sensible approach leads to a gloomy corner of the pain cave called "pivot hell." It's not because of the M (minimum) or the V (viable); it's because of the P (product). When we build an MVP and show it to customers, they don't get it. Because of course they don't: We're speaking in product language, but they only understand demand language.

As a result, prospective customers seem unenthused, and we don't know why. Accordingly, we might decide to pivot or build more in a futile attempt to excite them. Or worse, prospective customers may give nice but counterproductive feedback like, "This is super exciting! I can see how this would be useful." Or worse, "Have you considered adding X, Y, and Z features?" These comments are meaningless mouth movements uninterested people make to avoid an awkward conversation. We interpret them as interest in our product or an excuse to spend more time building additional features or adding new product lines. As a result, we overbuild the wrong thing and wind up in the pain cave, even when we're following the methodology perfectly.

We need to build minimum viable supply, rather than a minimum viable product. Let's go back to earlier in this chapter: "Help us identify low-quality calls so we can fix our AI agent, without all the manual work we're currently doing." If this is demand, what could our supply be? It could be a big software tool that has a ton of advanced features and functionality that promise the future of voice observability. Or it could be a simple tool that customers don't even need to log into, that sends the customer an email every time there's a low-quality call with some information. The simple tool doesn't even need to be software; it could just be a person listening to all the calls and sending emails manually.

In my case, I thought customers wanted "a new employee recruitment tool." But that wasn't demand, that was my product idea—and the minimum viable version of that product idea would have taken months to build and would have overwhelmed my potential buyers. I realized that customers really wanted "a no-effort way to recruit additional employees," which meant that building a big fancy platform would have been a bad fit for their demand. Keeping it simple and low tech was not *just* minimum viable supply and something to apologize for; it was actually the right fit for their PULL.

So now, the two questions I ask myself when trying to figure out minimum viable supply are:

1. What do I think their demand is? What is their PULL?
2. How can I deliver supply that fits their PULL with the least amount of time locked in a room building something they might not want?

These two questions led me to waste the least amount of effort building irrelevant things. Often, the answer to question number 2 is: "I can do this manually as a consulting project." Which means I can then go out into the world with a few slides to start trying to sell a consulting project, rather than spending a lot of time trying to build a product in hopes that customers will want it. Doing this is a great way to bootstrap a company. My costs are much lower because I don't hire a team and squirrel away building a product for months; instead, I can just sell a service with a few slides. When I do this, I seem to be able to charge a lot more and buyers buy faster. Why? In a final twist of "nobody wants your product," buyers can often get approval to buy a service faster than they can to buy software, and they expect to pay more for something they perceive as a consulting project or a human service than for something they perceive to be a simple software tool. (To add insult to injury: Buyers often have more patience and lower expectations for something they perceive to be a service!)

If I'm not sure exactly what supply I need to deliver, I can offer multiple supply options to potential customers who have PULL and see how they respond. Based on buyers' responses and actions, I can figure out what my supply needs to be.

How Do We Differentiate?

Differentiation is a fun topic because there is an infinite number of ways to differentiate that sound compelling but don't matter—or are repulsive—to customers. The PULL framework makes finding your differentiation vector less error prone. Here are two ways to differentiate when using the PULL framework:

- **P plus U:** "Everyone else thinks you're trying to accomplish X, but we know that you're really trying to accomplish Y. As a result, we have designed our product differently."
- **L plus L:** "Everything else on the market that's designed to help you accomplish X is limited because of Y reason. We offer the only Y-free solution."

These two approaches to differentiation are straightforward and don't require any ayahuasca-fueled "creativity retreats" or expensive branding exercises, though those may come later, when we've found real PULL and can focus on meaningless aesthetic differentiation. And they lead to the big question about innovation.

How Do We Innovate?

Every fourteen seconds, someone points me to a (real or apocryphal) Steve Jobs or Henry Ford quote. With Henry Ford, it is, "If I'd asked customers what they wanted, they would have said faster horses." With Steve Jobs, it is, "People don't know what they want until you show it to them."

These quotes are usually attempts to refute the simple ideas of demand and supply. "Steve Jobs and Henry Ford didn't care about the projects on customers' to-do lists!" Instead, they envisioned a different future and convinced the world to embrace their vision. They built an objectively great and innovative product, and the market came to them.

Obviously, nobody wanted an automobile before the automobile existed. This is not, however, because an automobile didn't exist or because people mistakenly asked for faster horses. *Remember: Demand is supply agnostic.* The automobile succeeded because buyers' real, unavoidable project was something like "get from point A to point B," and many buyers perceived that horses had some critical limitations, which made space for the automobile.

Let's imagine an alternative universe in which Henry Ford created a "human transport cannon" that fired families at their travel destinations at 1,600 feet per second. *That* certainly would fit the criteria of being (1) new and different and (2) something that nobody asked for. But nobody would have bought it, obviously. Why? Because it almost certainly wouldn't have fit anyone's real PULL. (Fine: Some may have bought Ford's cannon as a means to blast their in-laws in the general direction of Venus, but that would be serving a very different PULL.)

Innovation has to *fit* with demand for it to work. Within the bounds of demand, our supply can be wildly innovative, but it has to be innovative in ways that help buyers accomplish their projects in better ways than alternatives *as perceived by buyers.*

Alternatively, many entrepreneurs want to do MBA-style analyses to find gaps in the market. This, too, is futile. If there's no relevant demand, it doesn't matter if *we* believe there's a market gap. There's a folk saying: "There's a gap in the market, but is there a market in the gap?" If there's no demand, nobody will buy. Prospective customers will say, "Wow! This is innovative and interesting! Congratulations on building it!" And then they'll get back to work, because they have real things to do in their lives. The gap that matters is in the PULL framework: It's the gap that buyers perceive because their options have limitations or are unworkable. This gap rarely has anything to do with the one we come up with on a whiteboard.

So then, how do we use the frameworks of demand and supply to define a world-changing innovation? It's actually quite simple. *Innovation is simply the art of delivering new supply that is a better fit for a given demand.* Innovation seems to take one of three forms:

1. Finding a new project
2. Reinterpreting an existing project
3. Finding a new way to serve an existing project that overcomes current supply options' limitations

Finding a new project is the simplest to understand. Imagine there is a new technology emerging. As I write this, the hype is all about AI and AI agents. A new flock of companies has emerged to build AI agents to do all sorts of different tasks, from sales to product development to customer support. Existing software companies are trying to figure out how to leverage AI agents in their software, whether to improve what they already have or to launch new products and services. As these companies build their AI agents, they run into new problems and dilemmas: They need ways to test their AI agents, for example, and the requirements for testing AI agents are very different from the requirements for testing traditional software. This is a new project that is emerging; there is an opportunity to create supply that serves this new project in a way that the companies building AI agents view as dramatically superior to the poor options that exist.

The same thing happens with every new technology trend, just like it did with the cloud-computing wave or the shift from desktop to mobile. New projects emerge. Entrepreneurs tend to find these new projects by tinkering at the frontiers of a new technological wave. Mike Maples Jr., the founder of Floodgate Capital, the first seed-stage investment firm, wrote in his book *Pattern Breakers* that he found that the most successful founders were the ones who *lived in the future and built what was missing.* This might sound like nonsensical VC babble until we reframe it to mean that these founders simply find new projects emerging at the tip of a technological wave. When a new project emerges, it's impossible to assess its market size with any kind of top-down logical method. In fact, any assessment of a market size likely tells us that the idea is too small. The market size for anything serving AI agents is, as I write this, tiny. It might stay tiny, it might overtake all software, or it might be somewhere in the middle. We can guess, but we can't know for certain.

The second kind of innovation comes by way of reinterpreting an existing project. My personal favorite story of reinterpreting an existing project comes from how the payroll software industry has evolved. Every business that pays their employees needs to run payroll. The business can do this manually in a spreadsheet or with paper and pencil, or they can use software to automate payroll. In the past decade, a few fast-growing payroll behemoths have emerged.

Payroll software has always been clunky, difficult, and, frankly, ugly. One fast-growing payroll software company came along and reinterpreted their buyers' projects as: "Make payroll and HR tasks more delightful." The company invested in beautiful screens and user experiences for companies and their employees. In other words, when the company reinterpreted their buyers' projects, their supply *became* innovative and differentiated.

A few years later, a new payroll company came along and said, "Screw delightful. Automate payroll and HR tasks so nobody has to focus on them at all." That company architected their payroll and HR software not to be pretty but to automate as many back-office tasks as humanly possible. The company's product was wildly differentiated versus the original clunky payroll software tools and the new delightful one because they interpreted demand differently. Their understanding of demand and architecting of supply has enabled their product to expand well beyond payroll to handle other administrative tasks like IT's device management, finance's expense management, and more. This software company has designed its product so that it naturally handles such breadth; others cannot follow without essentially restarting from scratch.

My sense is that, as it relates to payroll, HR, and admin tasks, automation is a better fit for most buyers' true demand than "delightfulness" for all but tiny companies. The company that has interpreted demand as automation is building a differentiated product that is a better fit for what turns out to be a huge segment of the market. Its business is massive and growing rapidly as a result of this.

The third kind of innovation, delivering new supply for an existing project that overcomes current supply limitations, is often made possible by new technologies. For example, financial advisors are required to maintain records of all their client meetings. Their demand was something like: "Spend the least amount of time taking notes in order to meet regulations." Before AI, their best supply option was to take notes manually. It didn't fit their demand particularly well, but there weren't other options. When AI came along, the new technology enabled new supply to take shape that fit financial advisors' existing demand better, and financial advisors ripped it out of AI startups' hands.

Entrepreneurs often mistake this final type of innovation. The only reason this kind of innovation works is not because entrepreneurs build a "better" product or because current supply options are inefficient, it is because PULL exists—buyers' perceive their existing options as lacking or unworkable and are struggling against their existing supply. If financial advisors' demand was "Spend the most amount of time taking notes on client meetings," AI tools would have been irrelevant to them. They would not have pulled, despite the AI tools' ROI.

With these examples, we can see the physics of capitalism at work: Industries get closer and closer to buyers' true demand over time. And when companies stray from serving customer demand, as they often do, new startups can emerge and kill them.

This exact process happens even in your main street, brick-and-mortar business. Braden Weinstock built one of the top hair salons in Los Angeles, called efoxx HAIR. Customers' projects in high-end hair salons are straightforward: They want a great haircut and a great haircut experience, delivered by the best hairstylists. But most hair salons have very high stylist turnover—they simply can't retain great stylists. Braden's business partner—Eric Fox, a longtime hairstylist—came to Braden with a simple but critical insight: Stylists quit because of drama and pay. Braden realized that he could *only* serve salon customers' projects by serving the *stylists'* projects—essentially, *treating the stylists as his customers*. Braden explains, "As a business, our job was to build a home that recruited the right talent who would work together and thrive together. And if you do that, they will kick ass."

By reframing the project, efoxx HAIR did creative things that were nonobvious to traditional salon owners. Braden limited the salon's size to ten stylists, instituted weekly peer-led training, and supported stylists when they wanted to leave to build their own salons. As a result, efoxx HAIR became a magnet for top stylist talent. The best stylists wanted to work there because they saw the salon as a drama-free workplace where they would be treated well and supported even if they decided to eventually build their own salons. As a result, Braden was able to deliver on the salon's end-customer's project in a way that other salons couldn't. It just took a little reframing.

Whom Are We Competing Against?

The PULL model helps us think about many different sources of competition we face. Four examples:

1. **For this exact project, what are the other options buyers *actually* consider, and how do we stack up?** For buyers with demand, we often aren't competing against some other hip startup; we're more often competing against things like "doing it in spreadsheets" or "hiring an analyst."
2. **Which competitors are reframing the project more closely to buyers' true demand?** We might think the buyer's project is "make payroll and HR more

delightful," while their real project is "get it off my plate." In this case, we can get wrecked when a competitor gets the buyers' project right and builds supply that fits.

3. **What PULL is *upstream* of the PULL we serve and could prevent our project from becoming unavoidable?** In Campground's case, one could imagine a new service designed to help nonprofits prepare to fundraise more effectively, which happens to generate donor reporting as part of its service. Nonprofits prepare to fundraise *before* they get feedback that they need better reporting, so this project comes *before* Campground's project. In other words, this is *upstream* of Campground's project. If buyers have this PULL and buy this service, Campground's PULL could dry up to some extent. The interesting thing is that this competition looks vastly different from Campground and might not be something Sruti would traditionally perceive as a threat.
4. **What PULL is *downstream* of the PULL we serve that could cause our customers to leave us?** After customers have bought our product, they move on to what's next on their to-do list. The next thing on their to-do list might cause them to no longer need us. For example, as companies cut headcount in areas like customer support by implementing AI agents, they wind up needing fewer tools to manage a large customer support team. In this way, unrelated tools wind up competing.

So yes, competition is everywhere. If you focus on PULL and obsess over how PULL emerges in buyers' lives, you'll see competition coming from many different vectors, maybe even in advance.

SO WHAT DO I DO?

We know what we need to do: Find PULL and design supply that fits. What does the journey to PULL look like? Without understanding PULL, this is typically months to years of chaotic flailing, and then a random stroke of luck. When we understand PULL, we just look for our "hell yes" customer.

CHAPTER 3

THE PATH TO PULL AND HELL YES

Ryan Wan went from building a startup where nothing worked for two years—to rapid growth and being acquired (and able to retire) in under twelve months. At the time of his acquisition, Ryan was just twenty-four years old. (Adding insult to injury, when I told him I was turning thirty-two years old, he audibly gasped, perhaps surprised that someone at my advanced age could use a computer or that my nursing home had access to an internet connection.)

Ryan's business wound up working in an industry he knew nothing about; he had no particular insight or qualifications. His journey is common to every other startup story I've heard. It represents how startups get from "not working" to "really working" in the real world. It is wildly different from how I was taught.

Ryan's startup, CL1CK, evolved over time into something that was totally unimaginable on day one through the humble process of trying to find PULL and debugging (a nerdy word for "fixing") things that didn't work.

Years before I met Ryan, CL1CK started, as many companies do, with an ambitious idea. In college, Ryan and his cofounder won a grant from the Hong Kong government to pursue their startup idea, *a way for any website to optimize itself.* Imagine if, Ryan thought, we built something that would take in website analytics and automatically change parts of the website, using AI, so that more website visitors turned into customers. People would totally want that, right?

So, he built a business plan, raised money from venture capitalists, recruited a team, and built a version of the product. For a year, they tried to get people to use it via Google ads and all sorts of outreach. After twelve months, they looked at the scoreboard: Hmm. Zero users.

They decided it was time to pivot. Ryan saw that big Asian e-commerce brands were offering personalized discounts to potential customers to improve conversion rates. He figured that smaller e-commerce brands didn't have the tech to do this. So why not do the exact same thing but for small brands? These brands didn't have money for data teams like the big brands, so obviously they should want CL1CK's new product: a data-driven discounting algorithm they could plug into their website to personalize discount percentages and promotions for every user.

At this point, Ryan was accepted to a three-month startup accelerator program. At the end of the program, there was a demo day with thousands of investors. It was time to go heads-down and push to get as many customers as possible.

At the end of the three-month accelerator, they had one customer paying thirty dollars per month. Mathematically, this represented an infinite improvement over their previous idea. But Ryan and his team weren't satisfied, and neither were investors at demo day. Ryan decided that they needed to pivot again.

Next up, Ryan tried to sell an A/B testing tool to teams sending cold emails. Why this? They had already built a tool to run rapid A/B tests. It didn't work in e-commerce, but maybe it would work in sales. This time, they actually got customers. They were growing. But their customers were all different. They were serving sales reps, founders, and marketers, all across different industries and geographies. Nobody was satisfied; every single customer canceled within three months. At the same time, all the email providers like Google and Microsoft were cracking down on cold emails, which put pressure on everyone sending cold emails. This, plus the customer cancellations, was a signal to Ryan to stop what he was doing.

Which meant Ryan went back to the drawing board. Again.

At this point, his team was burnt out, demoralized. They didn't like what they were doing, and they definitely didn't like their results. The team had to decide: Did they just call it quits? Or did they try one more thing? After three big swings and misses, they knew that what they were doing was wrong. They didn't know *why* they were wrong, and they didn't know what *right* was.

And this is where Ryan and I met.

Before we go further into Ryan's story, you might think that Ryan is just a young kid with a bunch of bad startup ideas: *Of course* they all failed. But wait. That isn't the lesson to take away here. Ryan was thinking in terms of big ambiguous problems, pain points, and product ideas. He was, in his words, "stuck in supply-side thinking." Had he framed his previous ideas in terms of PULL, it's entirely plausible that any one of them would have worked.

But Ryan was taught to push his product, not to find PULL. As a result, Ryan thought that he needed to have a fully baked product ready before customers purchased. He also thought it was his job to do a bunch of research, build what he thought they should want, and then convince them to want it. These led him to overbuild the wrong thing, sell it the wrong way, and pivot endlessly.

So, in other words, Ryan got the exact same results all of us get by following the conventional ivory tower approaches: We confidently run face-first into the wall of customer indifference.

Here's Ryan's second act.

HOW CL1CK FOUND PULL

Ryan decided to start looking for *PULL*, now that he knew what it was. One day, he had a random conversation with his outsourced human resources provider. He had no knowledge of HR, nor did any of his team. He asked her what were the big things on her to-do list; she said, "Finding candidates for the jobs we're hiring for is really difficult. We have to hit our interview quotas for each job opening, and it's often tough."

To Ryan, that sounded like a project. "What if," he asked, "I had a way to help you with that?" He took his A/B message testing tool and showed it to her, explaining that it could generate personalized messages that she could send to candidates and get more interviews because the messaging was better, so she could hit her interview quota. It made total sense! To Ryan, at least. The recruiter was interested enough to bring her team to look at Ryan's solution. They looked at it and said, "Hmm, this is a nice-to-have." Ryan, who now realized that there was *some* demand here that he had just misinterpreted, asked why. One recruiter complained that she wasn't going to send these messages one by one; it would need to be automated. Another said he really didn't think this would move the needle. What they *really* needed was more candidates to reach out to. They'd tried a bunch of different tools and methods, and nothing helped. The group agreed.

This, to Ryan, sounded like it could be real PULL: They wanted more candidates to reach out to in order to hit their interview goals and had unworkable options. So he went back and built, in his words, a "janky LinkedIn profile scraper" for an open job the recruiters were trying to fill. It took him a few hours to do this, and the result was an ugly spreadsheet with a list of LinkedIn profiles. He showed this list of LinkedIn profiles to the recruiters in a second group meeting.

"The conversation felt different," Ryan explained. "The first time, when I was showing personalized messages, it felt like I had to push the benefits onto them. I was forcing them to read the messages. And they were saying *eh* and giving tons of objections. But when I showed the LinkedIn profiles, it was as if they were leaning in, pulling more information out of me. They looked at each LinkedIn profile in depth, explaining why each profile was or wasn't a good fit."

To confirm their demand was real and not just words, Ryan offered them access to his tool for a paid trial. They agreed! To make sure this demand replicated more broadly, Ryan immediately started doing outreach to other recruiters and recruitment firms. It took him a few days to figure out exactly what to say to get recruiters to talk to him. He eventually found that reaching out on LinkedIn and saying, "My company may be a customer of yours someday. I would love to show you what I'm working on," worked. Why did it work? Because it was sufficiently different from all of the salesy messages they were receiving from other startups ("Do you have these pain points? Our revolutionary AI solution . . ."), and there was something in it for the revenue-hungry recruiters: Why *wouldn't* they want to meet with someone who could be a future customer? Ryan scheduled ten or more sales conversations with potential customers per week, every week, and tried to sell to them as well.

Ryan used the first recruiter's PULL to frame the conversation with new potential customers. Using that recruiter's story, he explained how CL1CK's service helped recruiters get faster placements by quickly receiving a great list of candidates. It worked . . . sort of. Ryan sold nearly thirty paid trials in the following month. And then, almost everyone he sold to wasn't happy with CL1CK and canceled. Why? Because Ryan's candidate lists were, according to the trial customers, "really bad." This didn't make Ryan feel very good about himself. But he now knew that this feedback didn't invalidate his entire business. There seemed to be PULL, but *something* needed to be debugged. The solution came, as it often does, from a single customer's throwaway comment.

One customer was kind enough to offer Ryan a second chance. Ryan spent an hour with the customer, who said, "I know that on the job description it said the candidate needed to have five to ten years of experience, and they needed to be able to code in Java and Python. Actually, they only need up to five years of experience, and they only need to be able to code in Python, not Java." Ryan was confused at why the job requirements had changed, but he delivered a new list that met the recruiter's request. He gave the new list to the recruiter, who said, "This is perfect! Can we get more?"

At this point, Ryan had a thought: *What if the reason CL1CK's first list isn't good enough is out of my control?* The job descriptions recruiters gave him, it seemed, didn't reflect what the recruiters really needed. Which meant the way Ryan was describing PULL was setting him up to fail: Recruiters expected a perfect list immediately. This was impossible to deliver. This one recruiter had succeeded because he gave feedback and got a second, then third, candidate list. Could Ryan change his pitch so everyone expected to give feedback and receive multiple rounds of candidate lists? Could they thank Ryan for the first list being incorrect, rather than cancel because of it? Ryan introduced the concept of *batch-by-batch iteration* to his description of CL1CK's supply, setting buyers' expectations that the first batch would not fit their exact needs. Seemingly out of nowhere, recruiters had more patience. Ryan's clients gave more feedback, were less unhappy with the product, and stopped immediately canceling upon receiving the first list.

Ryan hadn't satisfied customers yet, though. He'd just earned the next set of complaints—or, more optimistically, the next opportunity to figure out how to satisfy customers. Recruiters, now satisfied with the lists, tried to contact candidates via LinkedIn and—didn't receive replies. They blamed Ryan. "What the heck," Ryan thought. "I don't control that. I never promised that. You didn't want my AI personalized messages." Ryan furiously tried all sorts of ways around this problem, and then noticed that one customer kept using his product and wasn't complaining about reply rates. Huh. He dug in and realized that this client was plugging Ryan's candidate lists into a different tool and extracting the candidates' emails and phone numbers. When they reached out to candidates via email, WhatsApp, *and* LinkedIn, their reply rates were acceptable. So, should Ryan just add emails and phone numbers? Long story short, he did, and more customers were satisfied. Ultimately, Ryan found that recruitment firms based in Malaysia were the happiest (apparently WhatsApp-based candidate outreach worked exceptionally well there), so he just doubled down on similar firms, and the business started growing very fast. Customers started renewing and expanding, not canceling.

As the above debugging sequence was happening, Ryan also cycled through business models. At first, he charged recruiters a small fee per candidate. This put the recruiter's project—get me more high-quality candidates—in alignment with Ryan's pricing—charge per high-quality candidate. It made sense in theory, but in practice, recruiters weren't happy, because they limited the number of candidates they requested from Ryan to save money and therefore didn't have enough candidates to reach out to. Ryan decided to switch to a "pay per job, get unlimited candidates" model. Then, to try to get customers in the door, Ryan offered a one-month, one-job paid trial. If customers liked the experience, they could move to a full contract. However, with this trial, recruiters would simply give him the most impossible job they were recruiting for—which didn't set CL1CK up for success. If professional recruiters had been struggling for months to find candidates for a particular job, was Ryan's little AI tool *really* going to conjure new people like a rabbit out of a hat? No, of course not. So Ryan changed the paid trial to a two-job, two-week trial. Recruiters still gave him their most difficult job, but they also gave him a less-difficult job and experienced success with the second job—which led to them converting their trial to a full contract.

The period from Ryan's first call with his HR provider, to PULL, fast growth, and a clear path to scale and profitability took about five months. By this point, every new customer was very happy postsale; each customer was running more recruiters and jobs through CL1CK every month. But the five months leading up to this were emotionally taxing for Ryan: "The hardest part was not knowing how far away the light was at the end of the pain cave." In other words, how many more walls was Ryan going to run into until he found intense PULL and was able to consistently make customers happy?

Even then, Ryan was still doing a ton of work manually. CL1CK's product was still just spreadsheets with candidate lists, though Ryan had automated the process of generating the candidate spreadsheets. Customers sent Ryan new job requests via WhatsApp and email, because there was no application for them to log into and submit some standardized form for new jobs. But Ryan knew exactly what the product needed to be, and his team was furiously building the right product that customers could use by themselves, without needing Ryan's help. Then he got a serious acquisition offer out of left field, which, at just twenty-four years old, he would have been crazy not to accept.

End scene.

WE CAN'T KNOW EVERYTHING IN ADVANCE

Ryan's business evolved into something that looked vastly different than when he'd started out. But he did this by, in his words, "running face-first into a new wall at full speed, every day for five months." Before we arrive at a general model for finding PULL and building a fast-growing business, we should ask: How much of this could Ryan have known in advance? How much pain could he have avoided?

In other words, could Ryan have avoided the customer complaints and series of existential crises and product evolutions? Could he have, for example, done some form of research, analysis, validation, and/or experimentation that would have gotten him to the answer faster?

Here, we have to be honest: Technically, everything Ryan learned *was* knowable in advance. Had Ryan known *exactly* where to look, he could have figured out that recruiters really wanted more candidates versus personalized messages, that they really wanted batch-by-batch iterations on candidates, that they wanted to pay per job rather than per candidate, that they really wanted multiple contact methods and AI-generated candidate "fit" ratings between one and ten—and a bunch of other little things Ryan learned that I didn't even mention.

But it's technically knowable in the way that you could have technically predicted every single word in this book: It isn't impossible, but it is so unlikely we might as well consider it impossible.

This is what makes the startup-building process so infuriating. Everything is technically knowable. In theory, there is almost certainly some set of seventy-three research and validation steps Ryan could have followed, and if he'd followed that particular set of steps perfectly, then drawn the correct conclusions from each step, he would have wound up with the same—hell, maybe even a better—business, faster.

But how often does that work in practice? Basically, never. Because there is an infinite number of irrelevant things Ryan could have also learned. How could he know what was relevant or not? It's more likely that Ryan would have repeated the painful LARPing cycle a fourth, and final, time. Instead, Ryan figured it out, because he knew what he was looking for—PULL—and just tried to find PULL by selling and delivering. *Everything that helped Ryan understand what his customers really needed emerged from the process of selling and delivering.*

This is why the well-intentioned advice that tells entrepreneurs to validate their business before selling—as if it's something we can do separately from selling and delivering—needs to be put to rest. This bad advice prevents us from approaching selling and delivering as our core learning process, and it gives us false confidence that we've validated our startup idea when we haven't.

So, instead of doing this:

Step 1	Step 2
Research and validation without selling	Sales

We need to do this:

Step 1 → Forever
Sales as research and validation (plus other research tactics as needed)

Unfortunately, when we try to validate without selling, our path to success always seems to look like this:

1. Start somewhere—with an idea, a vision from an ayahuasca retreat, a market analysis, a customer we want to serve.

2. Do a bunch of validation work following some smart-sounding startup methodology prior to selling.
3. Eventually, finally, try to sell and deliver something.
4. Get punched in the face by reality.
5. Obsessively adjust what we sell and deliver until it is right.

The problem is that most startups get stuck on steps 2 and 3. They think they've properly validated their business, and as a result they miss the signals from reality that their research was wrong. Step 2, in other words, prevents steps 3, 4, and 5—which is the real process by which the business comes together. These later steps are loose, intuitive. They sharply contrast with the rigid methodologies and approaches entrepreneurs are given for step 2. Smart entrepreneurs tend to follow the traditional rigid methodologies, and then when they don't work, say, "screw it" and just try to sell something, kicking off steps 3, 4, and 5.

Selling and delivering needs to be a startup's primary form of research. It serves, in practice, as the core process by which entrepreneurs figure out their businesses. It is the main character, while other forms of research can be helpful but serve as supporting cast.

To be clear: I wish this weren't the case. I will keep searching for an easy, straightforward research technique that actually translates to reality. Life as an entrepreneur would be a lot less painful if this existed. But basically every successful entrepreneur will speak nicely about popular research techniques, and then grudgingly (and quietly) admit that selling is the only thing they trust.

Even worse, we too often view selling as an unpleasant thing and use research as an excuse to avoid the discomfort of attempting to sell. Entrepreneurs, generally, *will find any excuse to avoid or delay selling.* I know I did. We entrepreneurs do not need more excuses to avoid sales.

So, if the startup-building process that makes sense in theory doesn't work, how do startups actually come together? The process in practice seems to be: *Sell and deliver the wrong thing to figure out what the right thing is.* In other words, sell and deliver something to find real PULL.

This is an accidental process—none of us does this intentionally. We don't think we're selling the wrong thing. We think we're selling the right thing, and then customers tell us we aren't. It's a brutal experience. When customers give us hints that we're selling the wrong thing, we often ignore them. Or we flail around, disoriented and confused. We often try to convince customers they should want the thing that makes sense in our minds and from our research. Instead, we need to take the information we're getting from our sales and delivery process and use it to figure out what the right thing is.

Every entrepreneur has a story like this. My story? It starts with this quote: "Listen, Rob. I hate that I'm paying you to help me hire new employees. I wish I could just pay to retain the employees I already have."

It wasn't the first time a customer had said something like this to me. At this point, I had onboarded over three hundred restaurant owners to our hiring software. One in three of them said something like this. I knew our hiring solution wasn't perfect, and I was worried that customers would cancel their subscriptions the second they didn't have to hire more employees. At the time, I had a bunch of ideas about how to make our hiring solution better. But I didn't know which ideas would work.

So I responded to this particular customer: "OK, let's say I build a product that helps you retain your employees. Are you putting down your credit card right now to buy it?" He said, "Hell yes!" I called five others—same response every time. We then built a new retention product, and customers loved it. This product was laughably simple: It connected to restaurants' HR systems and sent employees a series of automated text-message check-ins ("Congrats on your first few days! How's everything going?") to make sure they weren't quitting for dumb reasons, like: "I forgot where to find my work schedule" or "My uniform doesn't fit." This feature set wasn't even my idea: One restaurant owner walked me through his "standard operating procedure" that managers were supposed to follow to check in with employees. Managers just never followed through for lack of time and interest. We just copied his standard operating procedure (with permission, obviously) and automated it. The product fit PULL; we tripled pricing and our business direction got much clearer.

No matter where and how our business starts, eventually, it seems, every entrepreneur winds up selling something that's not quite right and using customers' reactions to evolve into selling and delivering the thing that is right. If this is the fundamental process by which we figure out our businesses, why do we need all the other complicated startup-building methodologies? And what happens if we do this intentionally, from the beginning?

FROM ACCIDENTAL PROCESS TO INTENTIONAL METHOD

If we are to formalize the process by which startups come to life, it is:

1. Craft a hypothesis of what you think PULL is.
2. Try to sell and deliver using that hypothesis.

3. Iterate based on what happens in step 2 until you find PULL and can repeatedly sell and deliver such that customers say "hell yes" and behave as if your product is irresistible.
4. Repeatedly sell and deliver as many times as possible, as fast as possible.

This method allows us to focus narrowly on figuring out PULL, using sales and delivery as the main learning battleground. On this path, I've watched hundreds of startups' journeys, and they tend to hit similar milestones and sticking points:

Milestone 1: Creating a PULL Hypothesis

At this stage, we have a *hypothesis* but haven't sold and delivered it in practice. Founders may start with multiple PULL hypotheses, but I recommend testing sequentially rather than in parallel. It's very hard to try to sell three different things at the same time, rather than going all in on one at a time. A common failure mode at this stage is creating a PULL hypothesis that only makes sense in theory and is not based on a real person's actual demand. Founders spend months suffering from a PULL hypothesis that only makes sense in theory, that's actually based on the product the founder wants to build rather than the demand a real person has.

Milestone 2: Getting Your First Customer

Some startups get their first customer on their first sales pitch. Most don't. Getting your first customer often takes ten, fifty, or sometimes even hundreds of sales attempts—even if your PULL hypothesis is largely right from day one. This is because you're learning how customers want to buy, what they need to

Milestone	Description	Where Founders Get Stuck
1. PULL Hypothesis	We have crafted a PULL hypothesis based on a real person's demand.	Crafting a PULL hypothesis based on the product you want to build, not a real person's demand.
2. First Customer	Someone actually paid us money! (This usually happens after we've tried to sell to 5–10 or more potential customers.)	Avoiding sales.
3. First "Hell Yes" Customer	Someone says "hell yes" before and after buying—they buy it as if it's irresistible, and use it as if it's addictive! (This usually happens after we have 5–10 or more actual customers.)	Not looking for hell yes (especially postsale).
4. Repeatable Hell Yes	We can repeatedly generate more "hell yes" customers! (This usually happens after we have 3–5 or more "hell yes" customers we can compare and contrast.)	Not figuring out what causes hell yes; continuing to do a mix of pushing and opportunistically serving PULL.
5. Scalable Growth Lever	We have at least one scalable way to get new customers. (This growth lever is usually only visible after we have a repeatable "hell yes" success story.)	Not obsessing over finding their growth lever.

understand in order to buy. Many times your first PULL hypothesis isn't right—maybe you're talking to the wrong kind of person, maybe you're using the wrong words and confusing her, or maybe you're just bad at sales. Sussing this out takes at bats and thoughtful debugging. I recommend iterating in batches of five sales calls, after which founders revisit their PULL hypothesis, targeting, and sales process. Many times founders simply try to skip this step—avoiding sales and hoping that their PULL hypothesis is so compelling that it will do all the unpleasant selling work for them. It won't, at least not yet.

Milestone 3: Getting Your First "Hell Yes" Customer

A "hell yes" customer is someone who really pulls, before and after he buys. Before he buys, hell yes means he behaves as if the product is irresistible. After he buys, hell yes means he doesn't cancel and might upgrade or refer others as if the product is addictive. He might even literally say "hell yes." There is no guarantee that your first customer will be a hell yes. In fact, I've seen a pattern where in a startup's first ten customers, maybe one is a hell yes pre- and postpurchase. Most customers are only modestly dissatisfied but will probably cancel. And usually, one or two of a startup's first ten customers are *very unhappy*. This seems to be unavoidable. It happens either because our PULL hypothesis is wrong or we make some mistakes when trying to deliver our supply. It's not good, and we shouldn't actively try to make customers angry, but unhappy customers provide a very powerful way to learn what PULL really is. Interestingly, as you find PULL, customers often seem angrier postsale for a while. This is because you're trying to deliver on a project they actually have to accomplish; there are real stakes, and they care. This stage is particularly prone to what I call "death by shiny object." It is usually in this stage we realize just how difficult getting customers to hell yes is, and our fairy-tale dreams of greener pastures elsewhere combine with the fear of commitment, and we decide to test out fourteen other customer segments and product ideas—and wake up months later with very little progress.

Milestone 4: Getting Hell Yeses Repeatedly

It is not guaranteed that once you have a single "hell yes" customer, you'll know exactly why she is a "hell yes" customer, or that you'll be able to *repeat* her hell yes with other people who look just like her. It often isn't outwardly obvious why one kind of customer is a hell yes and others aren't. This is a dangerous stage. Founders often assume they need to brute-force growth at this stage, hiring big teams and raising big rounds of money. Most of the time, their sales and delivery require a lot of push, because they don't really understand who pulls and why. Alternatively, founders who figure out the real reason some buyers pull and others don't can narrow their focus only to people who will pull, because these founders understand what causes a hell yes. When founders figure this out, they can use their "hell yes" customer's story as a selling tool. Entrepreneurs can show this success story to potential customers, and just by seeing the success story, potential customers pull. Once you have a repeatable success story, all that matters is repeating it. Which brings us to Milestone 5.

Milestone 5: Finding Your Scalable Growth Lever

Once we know exactly who pulls before and after they buy, our job becomes *getting in front of everyone who will pull, as fast as humanly possible*. In other words, growing or scaling fast. We need to find an effective (and, usually, cost-efficient) way to get in front of buyers. This might be cold calling with a sales team, it might be conferences, it might be writing content that brings people inbound. Regardless, we need at least one channel that can bring in as many customers as humanly possible. And this is how we grow from tens of customers to thousands; we hire employees, buy tools, and create artifacts as a *response* to one channel working, not vice versa.

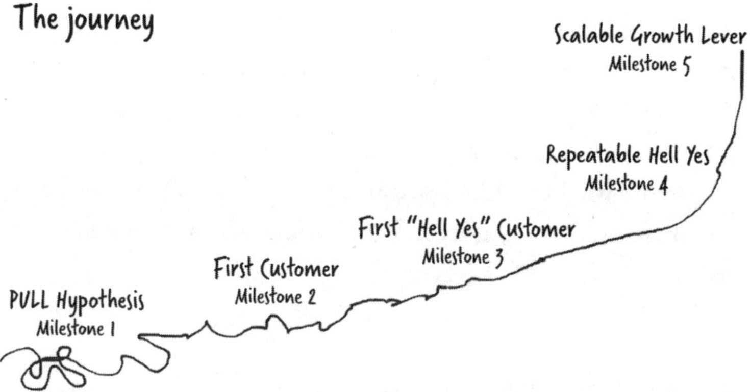

Some businesses get stuck on this journey or even move backward. Many times founders get distracted and pursue shiny objects rather than focusing on finding PULL. Sometimes customers' needs change or a competitor finds buyers' *real* PULL and delivers supply that is a wildly superior fit to ours, causing our once fast-growing business to need to restart from scratch. No matter what, the prescription is always the same: *Focus on PULL and getting to repeatable hell yes via selling and delivering.* Obsess over these things, and we have a chance of success. Lose focus, and we guarantee failure.

And as we grow over the years, our understanding of PULL—and what PULL is in our customers' worlds—will almost certainly change. Our product expands, our competitors evolve, and weird things happen like new "hell yes" customers who look nothing like old "hell yes" customers. We might eventually serve multiple different flavors of PULL.

At some point on this journey, we wind up becoming a known brand, and customers pull mimetically simply because other people they know pulled and it seems like buying our product would be a good thing for their career. And then we get acquired or take our businesses public and take home billions of dollars, and we don't forget our good friend Rob Snyder, who always believed in us and wouldn't say no to a nice bottle of whiskey (or a cozy villa in Tuscany).

Before we do that, let's see an example of how startups navigate these milestones and get from initial traction to a repeatable hell yes.

SPARKWISE'S PATH TO HELL YES

Vince and Romain, cofounders of a startup called Sparkwise, navigated from PULL hypothesis to customers to repeatable hell yes, following the time-tested entrepreneurial method: repeatedly hitting their heads against walls (more formally known as "trial and error"). Sparkwise's story teaches us how to figure out what our repeatable hell yes is—ideally without any concussions.

The two cofounders came up with the idea that became Sparkwise while working at the consulting firm McKinsey & Company. McKinsey is known for having exceptional employee training—the firm invests tens of thousands of dollars in training per consultant per year. Vince and Romain saw how excellent the training was at McKinsey and had a realization. What they believed was most effective about McKinsey's training—not the facilitators, but the participants solving problems together—could be turned into a tech solution that would give a McKinsey-quality training experience to companies that don't have McKinsey's training budget.

To test this, Vince and Romain articulated PULL and came up with their minimum viable supply: They would send a slide deck with instructions and activities to a small group of employees, who would then join a video call and work through the activities in the slide deck together, without any facilitators in the video call. Vince and Romain now refer to this as an "embarrassingly low-fidelity product." No matter: Two customers bought. Both were former consultants who wanted to train their teams on those business skills they had found valuable in consulting; Sparkwise had $40,000 in revenue and was off to the races.

Fast-forward one year. Sparkwise's founders faced two big challenges that forced them to rethink their initial understanding of demand. First, they were running out of relevant ex-consultants to try to sell to. Vince and Romain had already contacted just about everyone who had ever worked at any of the top three consulting firms, and alumni of other consulting firms didn't seem interested in Sparkwise's product at all. Second, when Vince and Romain looked across their existing customers, some were much more successful—and paid more—than others. Some customers bought very quickly and had intense PULL, while others took twelve or more months with lukewarm PULL. Some used the product religiously, others used it sparingly, and still others tried it once and never used it again despite giving positive feedback. This didn't seem to relate to how much money the customers were paying, which industries the companies were in, or how they'd heard about Sparkwise. Vince and Romain scratched their heads trying to make sense of this in order to figure out how to grow to millions of dollars in revenue on a shoestring budget.

This is normal—most startups experience something similar after they've gotten a few customers. And this is quite disorienting because you're getting mixed signals: Some people pull, others don't, and you're not sure why. What about your PULL hypothesis and business is wrong or right? When Sparkwise was in this situation, it was difficult for the founders to decide how to even describe their product. Vince remembers this confusing moment: "We literally went through hundreds of iterations. Did people buy because our product is engaging? Fun? Is it that we support remote teams? Is it that we're creating human connection? Is it that it's top-quality content? Is it that we teach consulting skills?"

Depending on which description Vince and Romain chose, they would approach their business differently: They would target different kinds of customers; they would use different messaging in their outreach, sales process, and website; and their product would almost certainly head in a different direction. This would have all sorts of downstream implications for their business, like affecting growth rate and profitability. And some paths might have been dead ends—things that sounded right, felt right, but didn't have PULL in practice. Or, they could have gotten pigeonholed, forever stuck in a tiny market.

To figure out which approach to pursue, Vince and Romain could have gone to the whiteboard and theorized for a few weeks. They could have gone "Rambo mode" and picked a single angle to run at headfirst. Or they could have tried to test multiple different angles at once, likely simultaneously failing at all of them.

Instead of these paths, Vince and Romain looked at each of their current and past customers, to compare and contrast their most successful ones with less successful ones, as well as people they'd tried to sell to but who didn't seem to have demand. They talked to their customers, too, and asked point-blank: "Why did you buy our product? What was going on in your world that made our product relevant?"

They created, essentially, a spreadsheet of every customer and potential customer in order to understand each customer's PULL.

Now, with this information, Vince and Romain could have tried to find their average—or most representative—customer. But this wouldn't have been designing around PULL. Instead, they focused on their best customer—the one who said "hell yes" bought fast, used Sparkwise a ton, and was wildly satisfied with their product. In other words, the one who *pulled the hardest* before and after he bought.

Even when Vince and Romain focused on this particular customer, there were still many different ways they could have described his PULL. So they figured out the "real" demand behind this customer's purchase by comparing and contrasting this customer with other people (customers and noncustomers)—some who had PULL, others whom Sparkwise pushed.

They were able to uncover that Sparkwise's best customer—along with their other highly successful customers—purchased when they needed to run live training sessions with their employees but didn't have enough experts on staff to run the training sessions. They had training needs their teams simply couldn't fulfill. At that moment, these buyers had an unavoidable project with unworkable alternatives. They desperately needed a way to scale live group training. Others—Sparkwise's less-successful customers and noncustomers—did not have this big gap between the amount of training they needed and the training staff they had. This difference between Sparkwise's best customers and everyone else told Vince and Romain what PULL really was, and this couldn't have emerged if they had focused on their average customer, or just any customer.

As a result, Sparkwise's new-and-improved description of demand and supply became clear. We can see how profoundly these evolved—*without changing their product*—below:

Component	Before: Ex-Consultants	After: Automation
What is their **PROJECT?**	Train your team like you were trained back at McKinsey.	Scale live group learning.
Why is it **UNAVOIDABLE** now?	Ex-consultant who misses the talent caliber at McKinsey but doesn't have the bandwidth to give their teams McKinsey-style training.	HR learning and development team that has more demand for live group training than they have supply of facilitators.
What is the **LIST** of options they consider?	Create your own team-training workshops on your own time.	• Hire more facilitators • Use a boring virtual training tool
What serious **LIMITATIONS** do they think their options have?	Requires too much effort.	Can't scale cost effectively while keeping the training engaging and effective.
What is our **SUPPLY**?	A highly engaging consulting-skills group-training tool that allows them to pick from high-quality prebuilt trainings and run them with their teams without needing to be present.	The only training software designed to automate live interactive training without human facilitators—and therefore infinitely scale.

They immediately started testing this in sales calls, at conferences, and on their website. They targeted customers who better fit this demand and more consistently felt PULL. This powered Sparkwise to $1 million in revenue, and then to land partnerships with the world's leading consulting firms and even power *Harvard Business Review*'s Virtual Group Learning offering.

When Vince looks at Sparkwise's demand-and-supply evolution, he admits: "Our initial success story wasn't powered by very strong demand. It makes sense why I often felt like I was pushing: Our buyers were managers who didn't have any formal responsibilities to train their teams; they weren't going to get fired for not doing the project, so it wasn't urgent. Also, rarely were they actively searching for supply to tackle the project. They would either do nothing or DIY a training workshop from memory. Sure, their situation wasn't ideal for a number of reasons, and they bought, but they definitely didn't have PULL."

Now, Sparkwise's business is designed around PULL. Not just that: Vince and Romain wound up articulating demand in such a way that *only Sparkwise* can deliver. If customers have this project, they would be weird *not* to buy Sparkwise. As a result, when the right potential customers see Sparkwise's articulation of demand and supply, they pull hard, buy fast as if it's irresistible, and use frequently as if they're addicted.

THE "HELL YES" CUSTOMER

The key to Sparkwise's success was that they went from a PULL hypothesis that somewhat represented reality to a PULL articulation that very much represented reality. Sparkwise did this by figuring out what their best customer's PULL really was and could only get to ground truth by comparing and contrasting their best customer with their other customers.

Which brings us back to the idea of the "hell yes" customer. This idea is inspired by entrepreneur Derek Sivers's popular book *Hell Yeah or No*. Derek's argument in this book is that we should only do things that we say "hell yeah" to, and if it's not a "hell yeah," well then . . . we shouldn't do it. The same thinking can apply to PULL and winds up being quite useful: *We need to design for hell yes, because if it's not a hell yes it might as well be a no.* Anything less than hell yes results in indifference, and indifference is death.

So what, then, are "hell yes" customers? They have two properties:

1. They buy fast, as if your product is completely irresistible. They can't not buy it and choose it over alternatives.
2. They keep using your product, renew their contracts, upgrade, refer others—as if they are totally hooked on it.

They might even actually say "hell yes" before and after they buy, which is always nice—but what is more important is that they behave as if they can't not buy it and then can't give it up.

Our goal is not just to find one "hell yes" customer; it's to use that "hell yes" customer as our blueprint to *repeatedly find and create "hell yes" customers*. This is how we grow insanely fast. We figure out what "hell yes" PULL is, just like Sparkwise did: By comparing customers who pulled with people who didn't. This way, we can understand what *causes* "hell yes" PULL.

The idea of the "hell yes" customer feels risky. We are designing for the extreme case, the rabid fan—rather than the average case or the mass market. The rational MBA in every entrepreneur's brain can't fathom the idea that designing for hell yes is, in practice, less risky because optimizing for PULL rather than push changes the physics of our business: "Hell yes" customers require less pushing from us at every step along their purchasing journey. When we design around PULL, we wind up scaling much faster and more efficiently than if we design around anything else. Finding clones of our best customers is much easier than trying to convince a bunch of people who don't have strong demand that they should buy, use, and be successful with our product. People who aren't "hell yes" customers often make requests of us that are unlike the requests we get from our "hell yes" customers, which leads to us changing—watering down, really—our product, messaging, and business so that it is a hell yes for nobody.

THE REPEATABLE SUCCESS STORY

When we talk about our "hell yes" customer's demand and our supply, we write what I call a "customer success story." Here's what Sparkwise's looks like:

> The HR Learning and Development team at [Company Name] had more demand for live group training than they had supply of facilitators, so they needed to scale their live group learning. They considered hiring more facilitators and using a conventional virtual training tool. These options weren't good enough because they

> couldn't scale facilitators to thousands of employees in a cost-effective way, and the virtual training options simply weren't engaging. Instead, they used Sparkwise, the only training software designed to automate—and therefore infinitely scale—live, highly engaging training without human facilitators.

See? It's a story with a beginning, middle, and end. It makes the customer the main character—not Sparkwise. This reads like a customer case study that Sparkwise would feature on its website.

The real unlock with this customer success story? Another prospective customer with PULL should look at this success story, get it, and pull. This success story is often the *only* thing a buyer needs to see in order to buy. We can choose which prospective customers to show this story to based on who "should" pull. And if they don't pull, potential customers can give us feedback on why the story isn't relevant to them. We can use their feedback to determine whether we need to change the story or whom we're showing it to. The task becomes finding clones of our customer success story, people who look at the success story and say, "Holy cow! That's exactly me!" Then they buy. Do this and scale fast.

Turns out, we can dramatically simplify the startup journey this way. It's just: *Find our one repeatable "hell yes" customer success story powered by intense PULL and then repeat it.*

Which brings us to the mind-bending part: Customers aren't really buying our product, are they? They are actually buying the *success story*. They want to repeat the success story. So a business is just the "factory" we build to repeat this success story.

If we want to know what to do next with our business, the success story gives us the answer. Let's imagine the Sparkwise founders are trying to figure out how to efficiently grow their business. Perhaps they're being grilled in a board meeting. Just using their success story, Sparkwise can answer basically everything that matters about their business—simply by focusing on repeating the success story.

Whom should Sparkwise try to sell to, and whom shouldn't they try to sell to? In theory, Sparkwise could try to sell to every kind of business that does—or wants to do—some sort of employee training. They could sell to anyone in the company too: a supervisor, a manager, a CEO. Any of these people could theoretically buy Sparkwise's product, if Sparkwise pushes hard enough. Instead, Sparkwise can just try to find the kinds of customers who see Sparkwise and say "hell yes" before and after they buy. Sparkwise would be wasting energy, time, and money if they didn't first focus only on these kinds of customers.

So instead of focusing on everyone who could theoretically buy Sparkwise, the team should only focus on near clones of their success story. This means they should focus on learning-and-development teams that need to train a massive number of employees but do not have the staffing to do so. There are a variety of ways they can figure this out, and a variety of signals they can find for when it's an active project at a company, but the point is: With a narrow target like this, Sparkwise can simply show these prospective customers their success story, and these customers should say "hell yes" and buy.

How should Sparkwise think about finding customers and growth channels? There are a million things Sparkwise could do to find new customers. They could do cold outreach, search engine optimization (SEO), podcasting, social media, events, ads, and a bunch of other things. Within each approach, there are approximately a zillion different techniques Sparkwise could use and approaches the team could test. This is overwhelming.

Again, let's start from Sparkwise's repeatable success story. If we can only do one thing, it should be whatever targets the exact moment when a buyer has demand. By this I mean: When a buyer needs to scale employee training, our approach should make it weird if he doesn't hear about us or want to talk with us. Perhaps Sparkwise writes a book about scaling successful employee training programs that they mail to every relevant employee who works at a good-fit company on their list. Perhaps Sparkwise finds some proprietary data source that tells them which companies need to scale their training programs, and someone on Sparkwise's team cold-calls those companies forty-seven times per day every day and stands outside that company's headquarters until someone talks to them (this might not work well, but you get the point). When our repeatable success story enables us to identify customers who have demand, we have seriously narrowed our possibilities by eliminating all the paths that would target people who don't have demand. As a result, we wind up with approaches that are highly effective for attracting and retaining customers.

Questions about their product roadmap and how to prioritize features, or their company strategy, market size, and how to sustainably differentiate, are all answerable via the success story too.

The success story encapsulates everything that matters in our business. And it helps us focus on the right things: We've often been told to "be customer-centric" or "work backward from the customer experience." These are clearly the right things to do, but because the concepts are lofty and abstract, it's not clear exactly how to put them into action. As a result, they have become platitudes said to muted applause at conferences. The customer success story, now, concretizes the ideas of "working backward from the customer experience" and "being customer-centric." When *everyone in every department reports to the success story,* that results in a customer-obsessed business by default.

The success story is the foundational model for startups. Here's how:

Question	Answer
Why do customers buy?	They have demand and our supply fits. The success story fits them.
What do customers buy?	They buy the success story.
What is the minimum amount of information customers need to understand in order to buy?	They need to understand the pieces of our one "hell yes" customer's success story.
What do customers expect after they buy?	They expect the results and experience highlighted in our success story.
So what does our business do?	It just repeats one success story.
What is our business?	A system to repeat one success story.
And when we have a success story that repeats, what do we need to do?	We should just focus on the system's bottleneck, as our business is a system to repeat one success story.
So what is the foundational mental model for building and scaling a company?	Use a success story to repeat, debug, and evolve the success story.
What else do we need to do?	Nothing.

WARNING: THE EXACT TACTICS DON'T MATTER

The next chapters dig into tactics:

- How do I build my PULL hypothesis?
- How do I sell?
- How do I debug when customers aren't pulling in sales calls?
- How do I scale?

I have personally used these tactics and seen them work across a variety of companies and industries.

But in the end, all that matters is we find PULL and deliver a repeatable "hell yes" success story. The outcome matters; the exact tactics we use to get to the outcome don't.

This is why I object to the boatload of complicated academic methodologies: They are a crutch. "We ran a ton of experiments!" "We analyzed tons of data!" "There's a huge market gap!" "We interviewed three hundred potential customers!" *Who cares?* If the process doesn't turn up PULL and a repeatable success story, it doesn't matter. We either find PULL or we don't. End of story.

Even the tactics I share in the coming chapters can be used as a crutch: Founders say, "We've had three hundred sales calls this year!" or "I'm having ten sales calls per week!" as if that matters. It doesn't.

What follows is, in my opinion, the least-bad way to develop a PULL hypothesis and turn that into a fast-growing business. It provides a series of tactics that are most aligned with the outcome, but remember: The outcome is what matters. Capitalism gives no participation trophies; there are no points for style or effort. If you're not succeeding, you haven't found PULL yet, and all that matters is finding PULL, by any means necessary.

PART II

TACTICS

CHAPTER 4

EARNING YOUR PULL HYPOTHESIS

A PULL hypothesis is a testable claim about reality: I believe that *this* person is prioritizing this project right now and considers *these options* but thinks her options have *these limitations*. Without a PULL hypothesis, we wander aimlessly. With a PULL hypothesis, we know what to do—talk to people who should pull and see if they do.

We've already covered the elements of the PULL framework in Part I, and in this tactical chapter, you're going to learn how to earn your PULL hypothesis. I use the word *earn* intentionally, because "crafting a hypothesis" sounds like something you can do on a whiteboard without knowing anything or after a couple of discovery interviews. Sorry, but crafting a PULL hypothesis that's any good ain't that easy.

We founders have a common pathology—we want to serve *everyone*, and so we create one big generic PULL hypothesis. Or we want to serve twenty different kinds of PULL at the same time, and so we craft twenty different PULL hypotheses. Even if we intellectually admit this can't work, we still do this. And so before jumping into crafting your PULL hypothesis, let's see what happens when we try to serve everyone, and then when we try to serve *multiple different types of PULL*.

Thilo, a Berlin-based entrepreneur, already had dozens of customers and hundreds of thousands of dollars in revenue for his company, Levity. Despite this, he was struggling with one question: How do we deliver supply for a bunch of different kinds of customer demand?

Levity's software product was what's called a *horizontal product*, in that it can be used by a variety of different shapes of customers. It allowed users to create AI-powered workflows without coding skills. Fashion brands were using Levity to have AI categorize their products based on pictures: Was this sweater green? Knit? A turtleneck? Startups were using Levity's AI to categorize emails in their inboxes: Was this email a sales inquiry? Or a customer support request that was sent to the wrong person? The list goes on: sales teams, HR teams, freight brokers, realtors, and so on.

Levity's customer mix left Thilo scratching his head. How was he supposed to grow his business fast if so many different kinds of companies were using his product for so many different reasons?

Thilo tried to create a different approach for each kind of customer Levity served. At one point, Levity was targeting fashion brands, sales teams, and dentists, each with their own website, messaging, and approach to generating new customers.

Levity's small team found it difficult to manage the sheer number of moving parts for all their different kinds of customers and their unique needs. Not to mention that each customer segment, website, and growth approach only *kind of* worked. Thilo felt like he was playing Whac-A-Mole to get any single one to "stop not working": Did Levity need to change messaging? Try a new growth approach? Or was there just not much demand behind that customer segment, and Levity should stop focusing on it?

As if that complexity weren't enough, Levity's problems didn't end when different kinds of customers bought their product. Thilo's varying customers expected totally different things out of Levity's product, which made it difficult for Thilo to figure out exactly what features to build. The fashion company, for example, wanted Levity to easily integrate with their e-commerce website. But nobody else requested this feature, and in fact every single feature request seemed like only one customer needed it. How could Levity's team possibly prioritize?

Because customers used Levity in totally different ways, it also wasn't clear how to price the product. As a result, Thilo priced Levity at a level that seemed equally inoffensive to everybody, but this meant their price was basically zero. At such a low cost, it wasn't clear how Levity would get to profitability or grow big. And every customer required a specialized onboarding experience. It took a lot of customized training and workshops to get any customer up and running. Finally, when customers stopped using Levity, they left for a hodgepodge of reasons that didn't give the team clear direction on what needed fixing.

Because Thilo was trying to serve many different customers and needs at once, every decision felt infinitely complex and difficult. What would the fashion retailers think? What about the indie developers? How did this compare to the new feature that seemed to be important to freight forwarders? Every decision had to be analyzed from about seventy-nine different conflicting angles, which gave Thilo a constant headache.

Thilo believed that *because* Levity had built a product that could serve a variety of customers and demands, he therefore *needed* to serve that variety. He worried that by narrowing down, he'd be limiting Levity's potential market size, and therefore wouldn't be able to raise money from venture capitalists who wanted to see massive growth potential. Turns out, this wasn't the case.

Thilo eventually narrowed down and dramatically simplified Levity's business to one kind of customer with one kind of PULL. This wound up being in the logistics industry. Levity's team didn't have a background in logistics, but their happiest customer was a freight broker in the United States. Levity's product helped this company sort through their many emails and attachments from other logistics companies to coordinate truckers and cargo. As Levity doubled down on this one customer's demand, they found everything else about their business getting simpler: pricing, product roadmap, onboarding, growth, customer success. All of these things went from complex to simple *because* Levity focused on one kind of PULL. In time, Levity's product evolved to serve logistics customers in new and different ways that customers raved about. This was only possible because the team was able to focus on perfecting one kind of demand and learning from it.

Thilo had feared narrowing would slow his growth, narrow his investment prospects, and pigeonhole him into a small market. Interestingly, the exact opposite of what he feared happened: Levity grew faster *because* they narrowed significantly. They expanded their customer base by a factor of ten in just three months. Venture capital investors were, of course, more interested in Levity because of their fast growth and ravingly happy customers.

THE REAL-PERSON RULE

If we can only serve one kind of demand, then it's really important to get that demand right. *The only way to get demand and supply right is to focus on one real person with PULL.*

And that's a problem because we tend to craft demand and supply focused on *anything other* than a real person, for example:

- A persona
- A group of people
- Everybody
- Our product or our startup idea
- Our vision for how the world should work

This latter path—crafting a hypothesis based on anything other than one real person—*seems* safe. It feels like we are reducing risk by focusing on a group, a niche, or an abstraction. It also seems like the appropriate thing to do if we are trying to build a big company. Plus, we can then share big market-size numbers with venture capitalists, who reward us with pats on the head and exciting investment term sheets. Turns out, this approach guarantees we get it wrong.

Here are the mechanics behind why focusing on abstractions like personas, niches, groups, or anything other than one real person causes us to fail.

When we do this, we combine what we've heard from a bunch of people to craft our thesis on demand and supply. We create a "person" by smashing together a bunch of different attributes from different people. It's like creating Frankenstein's monster. The monster might be made from body parts of individual people, but the monster as a whole doesn't look like any of the individuals it's made from. If we recognize this, we might try to make our monster represent the average person in the group—perhaps synthesizing the average nose, and the average eyes, and the average hair. The result might look less hideous than us smashing together individuals' different attributes, but it still doesn't look like any of the individuals in the group.[1]

And that's a problem because this monster can't buy our product. No niche or persona has ever bought a product, *because they're not real.* Only individuals buy products. Said differently, niches and personas don't have demand; only individual buyers do. And individuals only buy products that fit what they are trying to achieve at very specific moments in time. When we analyze niches and personas, we miss these individual moments of demand and *therefore miss the concept of demand entirely.* This is why salespeople tend to understand the concept of demand faster than marketers. Salespeople deal with customers one by one and can see it; marketers too often deal with data and miss it.

The problem with crafting demand and supply based on a persona or group only gets worse. The "person" we create on a whiteboard exists only in theory, a construction of our minds. And our minds are crowded with our business plan, vision, product ideas, and thoughts about how the world *should* work. Our minds are also, for better or worse, powerful. Powerful enough to subtly craft this "person" to fit our vision. No matter how hard we try to avoid confirmation bias, if we create an imaginary being, that being is going to be influenced by how we see the world. And we are going to wind up building a product or service for the imaginary being we want to exist. We're then going to struggle mightily to reconcile what makes sense in our brain with what reality is trying to tell us.

All this means that when we go to the whiteboard and use abstractions like *personas* or *market segments* or *niches,* we almost always generate something that resonates with nobody. Which is awkward, because the entire reason we use abstractions is to craft demand and supply that works for a lot of people.

The solution? *Don't create monsters in the first place.*

Dumb but true: In order for something to work for a thousand customers, it has to work for each customer, one at a time, one thousand times over. Our business *always* has to work for each individual buyer. There is no scale transformation whereby, someday, we stop serving individual buyers and instead start serving niches or personas. *How* we serve each individual might evolve to be more scalable as our business grows, but we never stop serving individuals.

So to nail PULL, we must start with one real person with real demand. This is what I like to call the real-person rule: *Things that work in practice are designed for one real person. If we don't design it for one real person, it works for zero real people.*

The real-person rule can bite us at every stage. An entrepreneur came to me scratching his head. He had many successful customers for his product, a tool that tracked analytics for AI features in software products. He was talking to twenty potential customers every week. Although he got positive feedback from most of the people he spoke with, no new customers were converting. He couldn't figure out why this was happening—until he realized that his company's real, successful customers looked nothing like the prospective customers he was speaking to every day. His customers, when they bought, were early-stage startup founders who were just trying to figure out if their AI features actually worked. Yet he was trying to sell to later-stage companies who already knew their AI features worked. Worse, the pitch he was using in his sales process wouldn't have resonated with any of his real customers. It wasn't about "figuring out if your AI features work," it was about something more abstract and theoretical: "model your AI features' reliability." So of course people nodded but didn't buy: The founder had fallen into the trap of crafting demand and supply based on what he *wanted to be true*, instead of what he knew was real. Once he realized this, he refined his pitch based on real customers with real demand, and targeted people who looked like them. It worked much better because obviously it did.

The real-person rule applies everywhere. If you're giving a talk, use the real-person rule to write a speech that actually works. If you're writing a post online, write for one real person and you'll write like an actual human. I wrote this book for one real person. (Hi, Ross!) On the other hand, you can tell when people *don't* follow the real-person rule. For example, this explains why car commercials are insufferably bland: They are almost certainly created using a sophisticated set of personas that represent "the upper-middle-class, style-conscious, budget-conscious, university-educated professional living in a coastal city." Their theoretical persona *loves* the car commercial that emerges; everyone with a pulse who sees it zones out. Everyone except for me: I find these abominations so offensive that I have to hold myself back from roundhouse kicking my TV.

The real-person rule also tells us how to figure out our PULL hypothesis, perhaps even without anyone roundhouse kicking anything.

FINDING YOUR PULL HYPOTHESIS

A PULL hypothesis, again, is a testable claim about reality: I believe that *this* person is prioritizing this project right now and considers *these options* but thinks his options have *these limitations*. A curious thing about the PULL hypothesis: It has nothing to do with our product, yet if our hypothesis is right, this person would be weird not to buy our product. Because a PULL hypothesis is supply agnostic and just a statement about how the world works, we should be able to find our PULL hypothesis out there in the world, no?

The way to develop a PULL hypothesis is to find one real person with real PULL. If you have existing customers who pulled, focus on them. If you don't have customers yet and don't know where to start, David's story will help.

David knew he wanted to go into entrepreneurship but didn't have any clue what company to build or what market to serve. He spent his two MBA years at Harvard wandering through a variety of startup ideas until he decided: "You know what? All that matters is that I find a customer I am proud to serve."

David went to work with a variety of potential customers across industries. He watched over their shoulders as they did their jobs, looked at their calendars, even reviewed their financial statements. He met with solar panel contractors: Nope, they didn't get along one bit. He met with fast-food franchise owners: Closer, but not quite. He met with independent physical therapy practice owners: Yes!

David then spent his free time with these physical therapy practice owners trying to build a firsthand understanding of them as buyers while searching for PULL in their lives. He tried to understand their psychology, their needs, their calendars, their financials. He met with them in person in their offices and observed them as they went through their day (with their permission, of course). In doing this, David tried to *become* his prospective customers, to see the world through their eyes. At one point he even tried to buy a physical therapy franchise!

I've found it hard, if not impossible, to develop a secondhand view of demand, where you try to understand demand based on what customers explain to you about their lives and jobs. You usually come away with a logical-sounding, yet wrong, understanding of their demand. Instead, by forming a firsthand view, you can predict how they think and what they'll do, because you experience the world as they do—you've built a theory of their mental to-do list that actually represents the reality of their everyday action.

Developing a firsthand view to generate your PULL hypothesis doesn't necessarily take a lot of time. A larger company was trying to launch a new product to realtors, and it wasn't going well. Michelle, the product manager responsible for this new product, had followed all the traditional advice: Her user-experience researchers had done over six months of detailed interviews, solution prototyping, and validation work. Her engineering team had built a minimum viable product, and she'd tried to sell to and onboard early customers. And? Nothing. Nobody used it, nobody wanted it. Her team members had conflicting opinions as to why this was happening. Some thought they needed more research. Others thought they needed more features. Yet others thought it was a problem with sales; they needed to convince buyers to want this well-researched, well-designed product. The team, as a result, just kept building, researching, and pushing. And it kept not working.

The product manager eventually realized that there was probably a good reason nobody was buying their product and why she couldn't even get realtors to use it for free. The reason just wasn't visible to her. Michelle couldn't see what demand *really* was, not from her cozy startup office, not from her secondhand view. She was sick of interviews and prototypes; she felt like she needed a firsthand way to experience what her buyers were experiencing. So she went and served as a realtor's assistant for a few weeks. She did whatever work the realtor gave her, while observing what the realtor prioritized. While doing this, she talked to other realtors every week to compare notes and see where her realtor's experience was unique. By week two, Michelle realized that the product her team had taken nearly a year to research and build was doomed. And she knew the direction the team needed to go in. Michelle's problem became a political one: Could she convince the team to change direction?

We tend to want to find PULL by sitting behind our screens, or scribbling on a whiteboard, or chatting with AI, or conducting no-stakes customer research interviews. This feels safe, dispassionate, scientific. It just doesn't work. We need to approach it like David and Michelle—trying to get as close as possible to a firsthand view, by any means necessary.

There's a saying that originated from Japanese manufacturing, "Go to the *gemba*," which instructs managers to go solve problems on the factory floor where the machines are (*gemba* loosely translates to "the place the work happens") rather than trying to solve problems from the comfort of their desks, data, and second- or thirdhand information. "Go to the gemba" emerged as a concept because even experienced factory managers need to go see the factory line firsthand to solve problems. When we're trying to build something people actually want, it takes a special kind of arrogance to assume we can build the right thing with anything other than firsthand experience, no? Imagine if a factory manager had never seen a factory. Is she really going to solve the factory's problem from principles on a whiteboard, without walking the line?

If we don't really have a PULL hypothesis based on a real person, then we need to go get a firsthand view of PULL by any means necessary. We need to go to the gemba—wherever our customers work. If he works from home on a computer in his underwear and doesn't want us to visit, we should find a way to at the very least do his job with him. Hell, get hired to his team if we need to. Work as a consultant alongside him. Whatever it takes to build that firsthand view of a real person's PULL.

This is why many entrepreneurs wind up creating a business to serve demand they personally experienced: We actually understand the project in the buyer's mind because we had the exact project on our to-do list and we understand its nuances. We have lived at this particular gemba. Other entrepreneurs start by building a consulting firm as a way to serve customers firsthand; many fast-growing startups are borne out of consulting firm owners finding intense demand in their own business or as they work in their clients' businesses.

We can also become our own customers. One founder I know built a software product for greenhouses. He wanted to sell this product to industrial greenhouse owners and had a fair amount of experience in industrial greenhouses already. But he wanted more firsthand experience, so he bought an industrial greenhouse and ran it for a few years. He used his greenhouse as the testing ground for his software product, but more importantly, he used his experience as a greenhouse owner to deeply understand demand and the other supply options. He didn't have to guess to get to his PULL hypothesis.

Another entrepreneur graduated Harvard Business School and immediately took a job making fifteen dollars per hour as an emergency medical technician. He found PULL at that job—*then* built his business. His story reminds me that the biggest obstacle standing between us and the gemba is in our minds: It's the mistaken sense that the gemba is beneath us. The past century of corporate managerialism has, in effect if not in intent, made it clear that selling, serving customers, and spending time on the factory line are for the unwashed hordes; we enlightened elite adjust spreadsheets and debate slogans and review slide decks in conference rooms. That this has hollowed out our industrial base, stagnated our economy, and made our managerial class wildly confident yet totally wrong is beside the point. It's preventing you from finding PULL now; go to the damn gemba.

GET UNSTUCK WITH A PULL HYPOTHESIS

Phil Green is the head of B2B startup advising at Harvard Innovation Labs (called the i-lab on campus). The i-lab is the university's hub for startups that serves entrepreneurs from Harvard's many schools including Harvard Business School, Harvard College, Harvard Medical School, and even Harvard Divinity School. Before this, Phil served in every C-level role imaginable in a technology company (CEO, CTO, COO), and he was even an early product manager on Microsoft's Word for Windows. Phil was a Harvard undergrad and Harvard MBA, as he often jokes, "back in the Stone Ages."

Phil joined the i-lab to give back and help student entrepreneurs find success faster. But in his first years at Harvard, he noticed that student entrepreneurs often seemed stuck. They were stuck in slide decks, spreadsheets, and endless customer interviews. They always felt like they needed to do more things before they could turn their ideas into action, no matter what advice Phil gave them to the contrary.

I showed Phil PULL and the success story. He immediately got it. It was, in his mind, a way for Harvard entrepreneurs to get out of idea mode fast. More importantly, it gave them immediate clarity on what mattered from their customers' points of view. Simple, elegant, effective.

After writing just one PULL hypothesis based on one real person, students could start engaging with potential customers immediately. They would get unstuck in all of fifteen minutes, rather than what one i-lab entrepreneur described as "the most brutal few months of my life trying to figure out a million things in my brain."

Sure, if students only created a PULL hypothesis, they might not have a bulletproof investor pitch or a ten-year business plan, but their prospective customers didn't care about these things. Their prospective customers cared about themselves: their projects, their goals, their jobs, their lives. Plus, Harvard students, and entrepreneurs generally, have a comparatively easy time spinning their ideas into big investor pitches and long-term plans. Additionally, these plans and pitches get much easier once teams have traction and real customer success stories.

Phil and I ran a one-day workshop over the summer for the i-lab. Students crafted their PULL hypotheses, got our feedback on them, and started doing outreach to potential customers to have conversations focused on debugging their PULL hypotheses. The workshop was well attended and well reviewed, which is great. More importantly, students made a ton of progress over the summer. One workshop attendee secured four big paid enterprise customer contracts in a few months, *before* he built his product.

DON'T GET PIGEONHOLED

When entrepreneurs hear that they need to develop a PULL hypothesis based on one real person's demand, they always conjure one scary objection: How do I avoid getting pigeonholed into a business that only serves one person? Or, in other words: How do I avoid getting stuck at a local maximum, rather than building the global optimum?

I, for example, wasted a year going heads-down and building the perfect supply for a single pilot customer's demand. I built a product that was a perfect fit to this one customer and nobody else. And I can attest, getting pigeonholed is brutal.

But PULL only exists at the individual level, so we have to find it based on one real person. Avoiding getting pigeonholed is all about what you do after you develop a PULL hypothesis. Do you squirrel away and build a product for one person, never talking to anyone else?

Back to David, who created the startup serving physical therapists. When he thought he'd found PULL in the life of a single physical therapy practice owner, David quickly created a slide deck and tried to sell a (not-yet-real) supply to other potential customers. His goal was to get five customers to sign up *before* building anything. David's first couple of slide decks didn't go over well; he iterated until he went five-for-five and felt PULL. When he found PULL five times over using the exact same messaging, he knew he was onto something—and he avoided getting pigeonholed into something that only made sense for one customer.

When we're worried about getting pigeonholed, we often try to test multiple PULL hypotheses in parallel. A friend tried A/B testing two PULL hypotheses for his startup; after conducting three hundred sales calls, he was *more* confused about which success story to pick than he had been when just starting out. He eventually said, "Screw it, I feel like PULL hypothesis A is probably right," and went all in on that one. He then figured it out and quickly closed his startup's first $100,000 in revenue. My experience is similar; testing multiple hypotheses in parallel seems to almost guarantee we can't invest the brainpower in figuring out any one PULL hypothesis. My general recommendation is to test PULL hypotheses sequentially, rather than in parallel. If you're struggling to prioritize which PULL hypothesis to test first, your intuition probably is to create a big fancy spreadsheet with all sorts of ranking criteria. I've found that asking the question Which of these hypotheses would I bet my life on? generates a better answer than even the most sophisticated spreadsheet. By some law of nature I can't yet explain, the act of creating a highly logical spreadsheet to rank startup ideas seems to always result in the worst ideas rising to the top.

But I digress. Now that we've found PULL in the wild and crafted our PULL hypothesis, how do we test PULL? Or, said differently, how do we sell?

CHAPTER 5

HOW TO SELL

THE PULL METHOD

I gave my first public speech as an entrepreneur at a fast-food brand's conference. We had scaled past our first million dollars in revenue, and although we didn't quite understand *why* we were succeeding (this was long before I understood PULL and figured out the PULL framework), we figured that we could grow even faster if we could successfully pitch our product at conferences for owners of fast-food franchises. I had spent weeks tailoring my presentation. The stakes were high: This was a brand where our startup had an opportunity to grow quickly, and this conference brought together the "who's who" of decision-makers within the brand. They only came together like this once per year. If I swung and missed, it wasn't clear I would get another shot.

So I came out swinging. My slides were well designed; the argument was sound. I gave what I thought was a compelling pitch. I talked about the future, emerging trends, and best practices. If they agreed with the logic, they couldn't help but buy our product.

The talk went so poorly that now, nearly six years later, I start to sweat thinking about it.

It was a ten-minute talk, but conference attendees stopped listening in the first minute. They cared so little that not only did they pull out their phones and computers, but they also started loud conversations with one another during my talk. I felt like a stand-up comic bombing onstage and getting jeered. But unlike a stand-up comic, I had no clue that bombing this hard was even a possibility when I went onstage.

As I walked off the stage, mortified, the next speaker stopped me. "Hey kid," he said gruffly, "I've done this a million times. That was bad. Try just telling a simple story next time." "Cool, thanks," I mumbled, then curled up into the fetal position and died.

Just when you think you couldn't have a more embarrassing experience as an entrepreneur, the universe conspires to prove you wrong. About a month after this conference talk, I learned the same lesson in an even more humiliating way. My startup had been invited to pitch our product to executives at one of the leading restaurant brands in the world. Some of their restaurants had started using our product. Executives were starting to consider whether there was a deeper partnership opportunity where they could roll out our product to more, maybe all, of their restaurants. If we landed this partnership, we'd be in the big leagues.

My vice president of sales, Jack, and I set out to craft the perfect sales pitch for them. We knew we needed something more professional than what we'd used for smaller restaurant chains. After reading up on a bunch of different approaches to sales pitches, we landed on one that suggested we needed to challenge our prospective customers to take action. In our call with the brand's executives, we asked what we thought were challenging questions, trying to get them to conclude that they *must* buy our logic and product.

Executives weren't challenged. They were offended. About three minutes into our sixty-minute presentation, Jack and I knew we'd blown it. The next fifty-seven minutes were a bloodbath. We only realized the full extent of how poorly it went when we later learned that these executives took our slides, gave them to another software vendor they worked with, and asked this vendor to clone our product. Which the vendor did. Yay.

Now, we almost certainly didn't follow this particular sales methodology correctly. And sure, maybe they were going to give our presentation to the other vendor no matter what we did. But I'm convinced that if we'd just told the success story of one of their restaurants, this particular presentation would have gone much better. And I'd probably look and feel a few years younger today.

Later, I joined one of our best-performing sales reps' sales calls and saw him using simple success stories to explain the product. Buyers got it, immediately—there was no challenging, convincing, or arm-twisting involved. That's when it clicked: The customer success story sells. Whether it's in a one-on-one sales conversation, in a conference presentation, or on our websites, we don't need a bunch of fancy methodologies or complicated frameworks to describe and sell our products or services. By showing our "hell yes" success story to prospective customers, they can decide if they want to repeat that success story . . . or not. In other words, we use the success story to repeat the success story.

START SELLING NOW, BEFORE YOU'RE READY

"When should I start selling?" the entrepreneur asks. The advisor responds, "Once you've validated your business idea with enough research. Remember, research is about learning. Sales is about pitching." The entrepreneur nods. It sounds smart, it sounds right; the advisor pats himself on the back. The entrepreneur will realize, months or years later, that this advice was the murder weapon that slowly killed her startup.

This idea—that sales is about *pitching,* while research is about *learning*—misunderstands both sales and research. It is, unfortunately, common advice given by academics and so-called startup experts. These are, generally, people who haven't sold anything in their lives. They don't understand sales, and they look down on the profession; they're teaching us, the next generation of entrepreneurs, to do the same—and fail.

Sales is a dirty word in much of the entrepreneurial world. In many business schools, sales is often an afterthought. When I was at Harvard Business School, there was a required marketing class but no required sales class; the startup sales elective was, at the time, more about sales management and sales metrics than about *how to actually sell something to someone.* (To its credit, Harvard Business School is adding more sales classes. Shout-out to Mark Roberge, Lou Shipley, and Frank Cespedes for fighting the good fight.)

As a result, founders often feel like sales is beneath us. In part, we're scared to sell and have a prospective customer smack us down. In part, sales feels too practical; we're supposed to be changing the world and doing things that scale, aren't we? And in part, we seem to connect sales with used car lots. Gross. Plus, if we find PULL, shouldn't the product sell itself?

With all these bad associations, it's no wonder entrepreneurs tend to avoid sales. And when we attempt sales, we wind up shooting ourselves in the feet unnecessarily. Sales, when done wrong, is about pitching and persuading. When we approach sales like bad salespeople, of course we don't learn anything. And yes, there is a lot of bad sales advice out there, especially on social media, that makes it seem like sales is all about persuasion, negotiation, arm wrestling, and creating false urgency. These are all push-based approaches to sales that make little sense when you understand demand.

No halfway decent salesperson thinks sales is primarily about pitching and persuading, though. Sales is about listening to prospective customers. Why are they considering changing? What exactly are they trying to accomplish? What does success look like to them? What options are they considering? How are they comparing and contrasting their options? Are we a good fit to help them accomplish their project? That sounds like learning to me.

So, dear entrepreneur: When exactly should we start selling? *As soon as we have a PULL hypothesis,* before we feel "ready" to sell. Selling is the most important form of research we can do. And we can do it in parallel with other forms of research. Why not start?

You don't know how to sell? You've read a bunch of advice about sales from either startup "experts" or sales bros, and as a result you're nervous about selling? I was in your exact situation. I am the ultimate introvert, and the idea of putting myself *out there* to pitch and sell and face rejection was so uncomfortable that I avoided it like Neo avoided bullets in *The Matrix*. I am still a mega-introvert, but I'm no longer scared of sales, because I have a totally different way to think about it. This chapter is the guide to sales I wish someone had given to me when I was just starting out.

WHY ONE-TO-ONE SALES?

"There's no way on Earth I'd pay you that much for your product," the prospective customer said. Parker's heart sank. He'd spent fifteen months in the pain cave and finally decided to just try to sell something. He'd walked this prospective customer through a PULL hypothesis, and at the end of his presentation, Parker explained the pricing. And based on the customer's visceral reaction, something wasn't right.

But the prospective customer continued, "The only way I'd pay you that much for your product is if it also did these three things." The three things he mentioned weren't difficult. Parker's small team could quickly add them to their product. "Seriously?" Parker responded. "So let's say I go add those three features to our product. You'll buy it then?" "Damn straight I will," was the response. Two weeks later, Parker's startup, Jump, had its first customer.

If Parker had tried to sell Jump's product *without* talking to this prospective customer—say, by trying to get them to buy based on clicking an advertisement and looking at Jump's website—what would have happened? The would-be-customer would have clicked on Jump's ad, looked at Jump's website, and—not bought. Or the customer would have received an email about Jump and—deleted it. To me, this hypothetical feels like a horror movie. I imagine Parker scratching his head looking at the data. Scribbling on a whiteboard trying to make sense of it. Coming up with fourteen potential reasons it's not working, none of them anywhere close to the real reason. He decides to pivot the business or something equally idiotic. I, an audience member in this hypothetical horror movie, scream at Parker, "Just try to sell it to one customer! You're so close!" In the horror movie, he doesn't hear me, and he digs himself a deeper hole into the pain cave, never to emerge.

(In real life, Parker learned from that uncomfortable sales call and built Jump into an insanely fast-growing company around PULL.)

This is why I always try to start with one-to-one sales, no matter what I'm selling. If it doesn't work one to one, it won't work at scale for reasons we won't be able to see or understand. When we sell one to one, we see customers' reactions as they consider buying, and we get their questions or objections as they think about it. Often, we hear them misinterpret what we're selling. This information helps us figure out what the right thing is and who the right customer is. As we learn these things and reach our "hell yes" repeatable success story, we can eventually graduate to more scalable growth approaches. But early on we want as much data as we can get, which means we want to have one-on-one sales conversations—and then one-on-one product or service implementations.

THE PULL METHOD: HOW TO SELL WITHOUT PUSHING

Varsha, cofounder of Offstream, dreaded sales. Like me, she had learned to follow a traditional approach to sales calls. She would probe buyers for their problems and pain points and then try to pivot to a presentation and/or product demonstration and try to convince them to buy. Not only was this uncomfortable for both sides; it also wasn't effective.

When Varsha learned about demand and the success story, she realized that her job was not to persuade prospective customers to buy Offstream, to convince them of her vision of the future, or to show them all her product's features and benefits. Her job was simply to figure out if the prospective customer had demand and, if so, help them assess if Offstream's supply was a good fit.

Varsha doesn't control whether or not her prospective customers have an urgent project on their to-do list. If customers had a relevant project, they would pull for more information about how Offstream could help them make progress on their project. If their project fit Offstream's success story, they would be weird not to buy Offstream's product. If prospective customers didn't have a relevant project, nothing Varsha could say would change that. A call where the prospective customer had no demand became a traditional research call: Varsha would learn about which projects they were urgently prioritizing and why; prospective customers would learn about when and why companies similar to them had prioritized the particular project Offstream helped with.

In Varsha's mind now, *there is no such thing as a sales call,* at least not as we're traditionally taught to think about a sales call. If buyers have demand, it is a "help them make progress on their project" call, or a "help them buy" call. If they don't have demand, it's a "research" call. Said differently, Varsha doesn't get to decide whether a call is a sales call or not. The prospective customer does. Sales calls, then, aren't the high-stakes, high-pressure pitches and negotiations we imagine they are.

These realizations lead to a sales methodology designed around PULL and the success story that doesn't feel salesy. The success story sales call is just a conversation where it feels like we are sitting on the same side of the table as our prospective customers. We're both looking at the success story, having a conversation about the success story, seeing what is and isn't relevant to them in our success story.

The conversation starts on the demand side of the success story: "Here's the project someone just like you had on their to-do list and it was their urgent priority. What's on *your* to-do list?" We have a conversation where we learn what is on *this* prospective customer's to-do list and why.

Then we jump into the options our success story looked into: "When they had to accomplish this project, here are the options they explored and the things they tried. Which options are you trying or considering?" We have an interesting conversation about solutions the customer has tried, how he thinks about his choices, and what's missing. We talk more about what success looks like to him and then offer to show how our supply option helped the success story customer.

In other words, we have a conversation that walks through each letter of the PULL framework: their *project,* why it's *unavoidable* now, the *list* of options they're considering, and those options' *limitations.* I designed the PULL framework this way to make life easier. If we're trying to get our first customer, we can use our PULL hypothesis and customers should get it.

Once we have a customer, we can use that customer's story. Once we have a "hell yes" repeatable success story, we can use that. The PULL hypothesis, the customer story, and the "hell yes" repeatable success story are all structurally identical, and so are the sales conversations you'll have with them. But as you level up to the "hell yes" repeatable success story, sales conversations get increasingly more effective, and you stop getting surprising new questions.

Our goal in any PULL-based sales conversation is to figure out this prospect's PULL, and in what ways her PULL is different from our PULL hypothesis or success story. If she isn't different, she should buy: PULL, after all, represents a person in a situation where *not buying is weird.* If she is different, we get high-quality feedback that we can use to debug our success story or whom we're talking with. More on the debugging process next chapter.

The PULL-centered, conversational approach is counterintuitive at first. I've watched hundreds of entrepreneurs' sales calls, and founders typically present to customers and try to convince each prospective customer he should want the startup's product, rather than having a conversation about the potential customer's PULL. When we pitch, it doesn't work, and we don't know why it doesn't work. Customers tune us out because something doesn't resonate or make sense to them, and they say nice words to us because they can tell that we want them to say nice words. After we pitch, prospective customers disappear, and we never hear back from them, never sure if it was a demand problem, a supply problem, or something else.

Instead, here's the structure of a PULL-finding sales conversation:

Section	Description	Structure	Shared Goal
Introduction	Before we jump into a success story, we have to make sure we both know why we're here and make sure we have similar goals for the call.	• Make quick introductions. • Confirm what their goal for the call is. • Set an agenda for the call.	Avoid an awkward conversation.
Demand	Before they can understand supply, we both have to make sure we understand demand.	• Uncover PULL elements. • Compare and contrast our success story with their PULL.	Do they have a similarly shaped project to our success story customer's project? If so, learn more. If not, what's their PULL?
Supply	If demand aligns with our success story, we can see if supply fits.	• Based on their PULL, describe our supply and see if it fits.	Does our supply fit their project better than their alternatives?
Next steps	If demand and supply seem to fit, do they buy? (Or take a next step?)	• Offer a clear next step, whether that's a purchase, an onboarding call, or a second meeting where they explain their company's buying process—who needs to approve, what forms you need to fill out, and so on.	Next step (e.g., meeting) on the calendar before the end of the conversation!

Which means there are really only three things we're looking for in a sales call:

1. What exactly is the customer's demand? What is their PULL?

2. Does our supply fit their demand better than their alternatives?
3. Do they want to take the next step?

It is that simple. How do we know if we find these three things? Well, ultimately, they buy. But we often have "happy ears," where we hear what we want to hear. We hear demand, when, in reality, the prospective customer is just being nice to us because we're enthusiastic. We learn that demand wasn't real when he ghosts us and doesn't buy after the conversation, but that's a painful way to learn. So here's how to tell if someone is actually interested or just being nice: Is he fitting it into his world now? Or is he talking about things in theory?

Section	What They'll Say If They're Interested	What They'll Say If They're Just Being Nice
Demand	"Yes—this is actually top of mind for us right now, and our options aren't workable. How exactly do you help?"	"This makes a lot of sense!" "This is a big problem that a lot of people are facing now."
Supply	"I definitely see this fitting in and solving our problem. I definitely prefer this to our alternatives."	"I can see how this would be really useful!"
Next steps	"OK, I need to bring Mary and John into the next conversation. Let me check their calendars right now. How's tomorrow afternoon at 2 p.m.?"	"Why don't you send me some information, and we can keep in touch!" "Why don't you email me to find some time on my calendar."

When he's just being nice, he's not fitting this into his world. He is speaking at an abstract, theoretical level, rather than imagining his life after purchase and how our product or service will fit in. He's not fitting it into a project he actually needs to accomplish. It's not real to him.

Given how important and counterintuitive this approach to sales is versus what we might naturally assume, I've found it's useful to walk through an example sales conversation, start to finish, that you can use in your startup.

SALES BEFORE AND AFTER THE PULL METHOD

Parallel's Sales Approach: Before the PULL Method

Renato cofounded Parallel after working in finance for another startup, Divvy, as they scaled from under $1 million in revenue to $450 million in revenue. Renato felt that the existing finance tools for startups were so complicated that even finance practitioners like him found them difficult to use. He wanted to make a financial modeling tool that was so easy to use, even founders without any financial background could use it. Renato pulled together an exceptional crew of cofounders, and Parallel was born.

Renato had the right intuitions about demand: Founders struggled to make useful financial models in spreadsheets. Yet they needed answers to questions like: When do we run out of money, assuming we hire a marketer in September rather than June and sales comes in at 80 percent versus 90 percent of our plan? These answers have serious implications for startups, whether they are bootstrapped or venture-backed: Being slightly wrong on your cash forecasts can be lethal. To add to the stress, venture-backed founders have board meetings where they need to be able to present different fundraising and hiring scenarios. The financial model is anxiety inducing. Parallel's product seemed like a no-brainer to Renato and his team. Their sales results suggested otherwise.

Renato's sales calls before using the PULL method followed a four-step process:

1. Probe for pain points.
2. Explain our point of view.
3. Give a product demonstration.
4. Try to convince them to buy.

In step 1, it wasn't hard for Renato to get founders to complain, at length, about financial modeling: It was tedious, it was annoying, it was stressful. Renato had uncovered problems and pain points, but he wasn't getting to demand because he didn't ask about unavoidable projects. As a result, it wasn't clear if they had an upcoming board meeting they needed scenarios for or if they were simply complaining. So Renato had no clue whether they had real demand or not and couldn't help them contextualize Parallel to their demand.

Renato would really lose the potential customer somewhere between steps 2 and 3. Founders would complain about how difficult financial modeling was, then Renato would go into a long diatribe about his point of view on financial modeling. Here's the exact monologue Renato delivered in a sales call:

> The biggest differentiator between us and your financial tools is we will build the model for you. We'll have a session with you to understand your business, when you tell us how you monetize and all your expenses. We don't want you to be building the model because you have far higher value activities. Second, our perspective on what forecasting should be is working backward from what the outcome is you want. So if by December, you want

> to be at $2 million in revenue, or whatever your number is, it's about working back from that number and saying "here are the things that would need to be true, spend would need to be X, our contribution margin would be Y." The reason we want to do that is because the value of a forecasting tool is telling you where to course-correct, so the goal is to say at the end of the month: Here are the expenses that were higher than what you were planning, and so what was off? Spend per customer? Customer count? And that way you can know where to focus, whether that's adding more customers or increasing spend per customer. So the big differentiator between us and every other forecasting platform is, we want to turn that outcome into a math problem that you can adjust and fine-tune along the way. What do you think?

Founders heard this and got overwhelmed. "I was hoping this would make financial modeling simple," they'd think, probably. "This seems really complicated, a lot of stuff I haven't thought about before." In fact, as I watched Renato give this speech to a founder who was a perfect fit for Parallel's product and who had just expressed clear demand and an urgent timeline, the founder talked himself out of buying just based on this speech. "This makes sense. . . . It just sounds like we might be a little early for your product," the founder said.

And if they thought *that* monologue was complicated, then Renato would dive into the product demonstration. Renato's product demonstration was an exhaustive walk-through of how his product worked: "Here's exactly how we build your financial model, here's where we track all your expenses and revenue, here's how the model looks in the background. Oh, and here's how you can really easily and simply run those scenarios that seem like they could be useful for you."

In other words, Renato buried the only part the founder actually wanted—a quick way to run a simple hiring scenario and understand when they'd run out of cash, for example—at the very end, after he'd waterboarded the poor founder with a bunch of complicated screens and financial modeling terms that the founder didn't want to understand. It was a testament to the strength of demand that any founder bought Parallel's product with this approach to sales calls.

Why was Renato so wrong? In short, he thought about the sales conversation based on what he wanted to happen and what he thought buyers should want. He wanted the entrepreneur to believe in Parallel's approach to financial modeling, to see how awesome and powerful Parallel's product was. The founder, on the other hand, just wanted to not look bad in an upcoming board meeting and to avoid running out of money due to a poorly timed expense. What Renato thought was going on in the founder's head was almost exactly opposite to what was actually going on in the founder's head.

Steps in Sales Conversation	What Renato Wanted Them to Think	What They Actually Thought
Find their problem	"Yes! Financial modeling is the worst! Tell me all about your point of view and product!"	"Yes! Financial modeling is complicated! I hope you've got something that makes it simple."
Share your point of view	"I get it, and now I see the world like you do, so I'm ready to learn about your product!"	"Dear Jesus, this is complicated. I don't want to have to think this much."

Steps in Sales Conversation	What Renato Wanted Them to Think	What They Actually Thought
Show your demo	"This product has everything I need! I know exactly how to use it!"	"Oh my gosh, there is so much happening here, my brain can't process it. Please make it stop."
Convince them to buy	"Where do I sign up? How do I pay?"	"Get me off this call so I can stop thinking about financial modeling."

Parallel's Sales Approach: After the PULL Method

To his credit, when Renato and I sat down and reviewed his sales conversations, he made quick changes. After he implemented the success story in his sales conversations, they went much more smoothly. This approach brought Parallel from near zero to $300,000 in annual revenue in a few weeks and has been tested on a variety of other companies too. MuukTest, Offstream, Jump, and dozens of others have gone from nearly zero to over $1 million in annual revenue in (at most) twelve months after implementing the PULL method for sales—after, of course, identifying real PULL and providing supply that meets their customers' demand.

Now that Renato approaches sales conversations using Parallel's success story, customer conversations are so much smoother. Buyers say, "Wow! It sounds like you've been listening in on my meetings!" Or more bluntly: "This punches me in the soul." While this conversation was mind-blowing for potential customers, it quickly got repetitive for Renato. This is a good thing because Renato was able to hire sales reps to have standardized conversations with potential customers. Demand and the success story did the selling; skilled sales reps facilitated the process.

I have found that entrepreneurs across industries can use Parallel's conversation structure and slide deck in their sales conversations and it works, assuming there's PULL. Even when selling to consumers, structuring a conversation this way works. Sure, we might not pull up a slide deck to sell blue jeans, but we can still use the following conversation structure.

Renato has a few core slides that mirror the success story framework. He doesn't use every slide in every sales call. The slides help structure and guide the conversation; they are not a replacement for the conversation, as you'll see in the transcript of one of Parallel's sales calls, below. Renato's four slides are:

1. Project
2. Options
3. Supply
4. Pricing

These slides correspond to the different parts of the success story framework, moving from demand to supply. The conversation is structured in four main parts.

Part 1: Introductions and Agenda

In the beginning of a sales call, Renato sets up a sales conversation with an agenda that's *based on what the customer wants to get out of the call* (not what Renato wants to accomplish in the call). If Renato didn't set an agenda, the prospective customer would have no clue where the call was heading. If Renato set an agenda based on his own goals for the call, he wouldn't know why the prospective customer had shown up for the call in the first place. Now, the temptation here is to think that setting an agenda is wasting the buyer's time and reducing the amount of time for you to show her how cool your product or service is. This is totally backward because we only know what the right thing to show her is if we understand why she's here.

Renato: "Thanks for taking the time to talk today. I'm excited to walk you through Parallel, which at a high level helps founders run financial scenarios without headaches. My name is Renato, and I'm a sales rep here at Parallel. I know you're busy—why'd you take the call today, and what are you hoping to get out of it?"

Prospect: "Yeah, I saw your email come through, and I usually don't respond to these cold emails I get every day. But I saw the thing about the financial model and running scenarios, and we are thinking about hiring a few people and I need to present a plan to the board, so I figured why not take a call to learn more."

Renato: "I hear that all the time. Based on that, here's what I thought we'd do today. I'm happy to walk you through how other startup founders use Parallel to simplify financial modeling and running hiring and fundraising scenarios, and we can have a conversation about whether it's relevant to you or not. Then, if you think it might be relevant to you, we can talk about how other startups have gotten started with Parallel. That sound good?"

Prospect: "Sounds perfect, let's do it."

Renato: "Great. Before we get to that, mind if I ask you a few questions about your financial model so I can show you the right things?"

Prospect: "Absolutely."

By setting up the call this way, Renato understands a little bit about the prospective customer's PULL, the buyer knows she's going to get exactly what she wants out of the call, and Renato has earned the right to ask a few questions to understand her PULL more deeply.

Part 2: PULL (Demand)

Every startup's sales process features a few questions that the founders and/or salespeople ask at the beginning of the call. These are called discovery questions, and their purpose is to help the buyer articulate her PULL. If we already have some elements of PULL from the question Why did you take the call?, we simply need to double-click on the other elements of PULL. If not, we may start with broad questions, trying to get the prospective customer to articulate one element of the PULL framework. For example:

- As it relates to your financial model, what are you focused on right now? What are you trying to accomplish or change?
- I assume you saw our website. What did you think was relevant to what you're focused on right now?

These questions evolve over time. In fact, I've worked with some companies that have perfected these questions such that they know with nearly 100 percent confidence whether a prospect will buy based on the answers to a few innocuous-seeming questions at the beginning of the call.

One common error I have seen is that we take this time to try to understand every single aspect of the buyer's life or business. Entrepreneurs think they need to understand the prospective customer's current state, problems, pain points, team structure, processes, and cats' names. These are interesting to learn in a research project, but remember, these things are *not* PULL. When selling, we need to fill out the PULL framework. Most everything else is noise, at best.

Let's see how Renato approaches this part.

Renato: "You mentioned you are planning on hiring people and are thinking about running financial scenarios to present to the board. When founders come to us, we typically hear that they spend hours wrangling with a spreadsheet-based financial model and don't always feel confident about the model despite spending a ton of time on it. I'll pause there—what doesn't resonate with you?"

Renato asks what *doesn't* resonate with the buyer rather than asking what *does* resonate. This makes it safe and easy for the buyer to admit she doesn't have demand; asking what does resonate gets you polite answers and head-nods from people who don't have demand—not useful information to figure out why they don't have demand.

At this point, Renato might show his project slide with quotes from founders:

When founders prioritize saving 90% of time and headaches on financial models

> "We have a board meeting next month and need to be able to quickly run through different fundraising scenarios."
>
> "We are considering hiring sales reps and need to model out our cash situation based on their quota attainment."
>
> "I need to have our model up-to-date but can't justify the time figuring this out myself."

Prospect: "Yeah, this is exactly our situation. I was mentioning earlier the hiring piece. We're considering starting the hiring process for some sales reps next month, and just figuring out what impact that's going to have on when we need to raise money next is really complicated. What if they don't ramp up and hit quota as fast as we think they will? What if they miss quota? Then trying to map when cash comes in versus when cash goes out is hurting my brain. I'm not a finance person."

In Renato's brain, he pencils in two pieces of his success story model:

Success Story Component	Answer
What is their **PROJECT?**	Need to run financial scenarios about what the cash implications are of hiring sales reps.
Why is it **UNAVOIDABLE** now?	Considering hiring reps next month and need answers before we can start hiring.
What's on the **LIST** of options they consider?	TBD
What serious **LIMITATIONS** do they think their options have?	TBD
Does our **SUPPLY** fit?	TBD

Renato could dig a little deeper here to try to gauge how urgent this project is. It sounds like the prospect needs the ability to run scenarios ASAP to make a hiring decision next month. Renato could ask questions like: What happens if you don't get this scenario right? When do you have to present your plan to the board? Why is your current financial model not good enough?

Renato: "I hear that all the time. Now, you mentioned you're still in spreadsheets and you haven't really considered anything else. You haven't looked into any financial modeling tools and aren't hiring for someone to do your financial model. What did I miss there?"

Prospect: "Yeah, actually now that you mention it, I guess I did look into a few of the financial modeling tools a while back. Honestly, they felt even more complicated than my spreadsheets, so I just didn't think there was any other option than spreadsheets."

Renato then shows his options slide, which shows four different approaches founders have used to wrangle their financial model.

Options founders typically have considered or tried

DIY in spreadsheets

Finance hire or contractor

Tools for finance experts

Missing: Something designed for founders

Renato: "That's interesting. I typically hear basically the same thing. And just like you, most founders tend to avoid the complicated tools for finance experts and delay finance hires as long as they possibly can. For people in that situation, where they've either tried or ruled out other options, Parallel is often a good fit because it's much easier than managing a spreadsheet and is designed for founders and doesn't require them to hire someone in finance just to manage the model."

Prospect: "Wow, yeah that's exactly where I am. This is exactly how I'm thinking about it. How does your product work?"

Renato: "Perfect, so just to confirm I've heard you correctly, you're trying to run financial scenarios to make hiring decisions you'll present to the board next month. You're in spreadsheets but can't run your scenarios there. You aren't ready to hire someone to run your financial model yet. You looked into financial modeling tools, but they were too complicated, and so what you're looking for is a simple financial modeling tool for founders that lets you quickly run scenarios."

Prospect: "Yes, that's exactly it!"

This is what it feels like for customers to have demand and pull for supply. This is a signal that you've nailed demand. In Renato's brain, he pencils in the list and limitation parts of his success story model and switches from the demand side to the supply side of the conversation.

Success Story Component	Answer
What is their **PROJECT?**	Need to run financial scenarios about what the cash implications are of hiring sales reps.
Why is it **UNAVOIDABLE** now?	Considering hiring reps next month and need answers before we can start hiring.
What's on the **LIST** of options they consider?	Looked into financial tools, hiring, and spreadsheets.
What serious **LIMITATIONS** do they think their options have?	Too difficult to use.
Does our **SUPPLY** fit?	TBD

Once we've found PULL, we've earned the right to describe and demonstrate supply. However, a common error pattern is a founder rushing through the demand part of the conversation because he thinks the meat of the conversation is the supply part, where the buyer sees his product or service. Don't do that! If we don't understand their demand—and then, importantly, confirm we are aligned with them on what their demand is—showing off our supply is likely to confuse everyone. Reread what Renato did at the end: *He articulated the buyer's PULL and saw whether she agreed or didn't.* If the buyer had said, "Eh, sort of, I guess," that would have been a sign that Renato got it wrong and needs to spend more time there. If Renato doesn't do this, he could have a totally different mental model of what the buyer's demand is versus what's actually in the buyer's brain—which won't end well. Figuring out the buyer's demand is often the longest part of the sales conversation. When you know her demand, describing supply that fits doesn't take long at all.

Part 3: Supply

For Parallel, the supply part of a sales conversation usually takes three to five minutes. Renato starts with his supply slide, which shows Parallel's product running a scenario, plus a couple of quotes from founders who achieved success with Parallel. It looks simple and clean.

> **Parallel: Financial modeling designed for founders**
>
> [Clean graphic of a financial scenario]
>
> "I now run scenarios weekly—for our board meetings, hiring plans, and fundraising options."
>
> "I feel totally in control of our finances now, even though I'm not a finance person."

Renato: "Great. Here's a high-level overview of what Parallel helps founders accomplish. As you can see here, the main goal is for founders to be able to quickly run scenarios on hiring, fundraising, or whatever—and be able to either make decisions internally and/or present these scenarios confidently to others. You can see here, all a founder has to do is click a few buttons and they've got a new scenario—rather than having to make a bunch of copies of your financial model or add new tabs to the spreadsheet. There's more, but I'll pause here. Is this how you were expecting it would work?"

Prospect: "This is exactly what I was hoping it would do. Wow, that looks so simple. But how do we get the numbers into Parallel so it knows what to do?"

In Renato's brain, he pencils in the fifth piece of his success story model. The buyer has just pulled for more information about getting started. This is a good sign.

A common error mode here is talking too much about supply and not pausing after a simple description to see if it makes sense to customers. Often, we ramble on for a few minutes only to see a faraway look emerge in their eyes. We have to play damage control in this scenario, and it's hard to win them back or figure out where we lost them.

Note that here, a prospective customer might ask a variety of questions to make sure Parallel is a fit for her specific needs. How does it handle offshore contractors? How does it handle exchange rates? How does it deal with biweekly versus bimonthly payroll expenses? Renato has a set of slides in his slide deck's appendix that answer frequently asked questions. At this point, Renato answers the customer's questions and takes note of any new questions that he may need to add to his appendix.

Success Story Component	Answer
What is their **PROJECT?**	Need to run financial scenarios about what the cash implications are of hiring sales reps.
Why is it **UNAVOIDABLE** now?	Considering hiring reps next month and need answers before we can start hiring.
What's on the **LIST** of options they consider?	Looked into financial tools, hiring, and spreadsheets.
What serious **LIMITATIONS** do they think their options have?	Too difficult to use.
Does our **SUPPLY** fit?	"Exactly what I was hoping it would do."

Renato [after answering a few questions]: "I want to make sure we've covered everything else you were concerned about. I know you came in skeptical about financial modeling tools being too complicated. Did we cover that? Was there anything else there you wanted to dig into?"

Prospect: "No, no I think we got it all. I get it and want to try it out."

Renato: "OK, so assuming the price makes sense, sounds like you'd want to schedule your onboarding session this week?"

Prospect: "Definitely."

Renato pulls up the pricing slide. This slide is broken into three parts: (1) what you get, (2) how others think about price, and (3) what you pay.

Renato: "OK, so let me bring all of this together. When startups buy Parallel's financial modeling tool, they get access to the software, integration into their existing systems, a white-glove onboarding process, responsive support, and more. Founders usually compare us to hiring a finance contractor or employee, which costs $100,000 or more per year, or financial modeling tools, which cost up to $10,000 or $20,000 per year. When founders buy Parallel, they pay [X] dollars. This is an annual commitment, but you can cancel if you're unsatisfied in the first ninety days and get your money back. Does this fit what you expected?"

Parallel: Financial modeling designed for founders

What you get:

- Access to the software
- Integration into existing systems
- White-glove onboarding
- Responsive support

How founders think about price:

- Other tools: $10K–20K+ per year
- Hiring in finance: $100K+ per year
- Parallel: Just $X

Plus: 90-day money-back guarantee

Prospect: "This is quite reasonable. Let's do it!"

Part 4: Next Steps

At this point, the call has usually lasted fifteen, maybe twenty minutes. Renato wraps up the call by scheduling an onboarding session, sending a contract for signature, and answering any remaining questions. The thirty-minute call concludes with time to spare.

So What?

Parallel's sales improvement isn't unique or an anomaly. It's a result of them having a conversation about the buyer's PULL and Parallel's success story, not just about Parallel's product. Customers don't feel pressured to buy, and Renato doesn't feel like he needs to apply pressure. PULL *causes* sales calls to go smoothly and deals to close.

Depending on your situation, you might not be able to close sales in one call. If your pricing is over $10,000 per year, you're probably going to need multiple calls with other stakeholders or for more in-depth questions about implementation. The way I think about it is there are two parts of sales:

1. The "success-story-fit" part, which we largely covered here. When we nail this part, they want to buy our product. Our job from here on out is simply to help them buy (sometimes this is easier said than done).
2. And then, the "project management" part, where we help our prospective customers through a set of steps they need to go through in order to get alignment and finalize the purchase.

These later project-management steps are much easier when they are *also* grounded in PULL and the success story: "Here's the process we've typically seen customers use to make a decision. How are you different? How do you plan to make a decision?"

Whether you're selling a $10 or $500,000 product or service, start with a three-step sales process that looks like the table on the next page.

If our product's pricing is low, we might not be able to afford to do sales one to one forever. But by doing one-to-one sales, we're able to figure out how to describe our success story so that prospective customers say "hell yes" to it. We can then take what

Step 1: Success Story Fit	Step 2: Deep Dive and Planning	Step 3: Onboarding
The example we just went through above.	A more detailed examination of whether our supply fits their demand. The bigger the contract, the more likely it is we will need to create a project plan with our customers to get to step 3; that includes things like, "Get contract reviewed and go through procurement" and "Show this off to a bunch of other executives and potential users." This part can take days or months.	I have seen teams successfully schedule an onboarding call as a way to drive a reasonably quick decision in step 2. Teams schedule an onboarding call during their deep-dive session(s) and use that as a forcing function to get the contract signed in advance. This is important because time changes buyers' priorities.

works one to one and use it elsewhere—on our websites, in conference talks, in webinars, in advertisements.

WHAT IF THE DOG CATCHES THE CAR?

What happens after someone buys?

We tend to naturally think, *OK, we hand over our product or service and that's that!* This is a mistake. We've just been given an opportunity to learn what customers *really* want to achieve by helping them achieve it. We should take advantage of the learning opportunity, while minimizing the chances that they don't succeed. I think of it as "forcing the customer to accomplish their project by any means necessary."

Delivery is another chance to go to the gemba. David Cancel, cofounder of Drift (acquired for $1 billion), would fly out to help his early customers use his software product, even though they were paying a few dollars per month for it. He just wanted to see them use it to understand what they were really trying to accomplish, what their demand *really* was. As he better understood this, David could figure out how to build the right product.

Another friend, Steven, did something similar: He was building a product for physical therapists (not David, last chapter, who *also* built a product for physical therapists) to use with their clients, and he decided he didn't understand his customers well enough even though he was at hundreds of thousands of dollars in revenue. Some customers weren't happy, while others were, and he felt like he couldn't figure this out from behind his desk. So he instituted a new rule: He would fly out to every new customer and spend a few days with them while personally helping them implement his product and become successful with it. He did this for over a year. Steven credits this approach with giving him the insights he needed to improve their product and sales process, and it also generated very happy customers and many referrals.

If we're selling a product customers should be able to use themselves, we should still deliver it manually and watch them use it in their world. Whether it's a vacuum cleaner or a software product, watching them try (and, often, struggle mightily) to use it in their world gives us clear signals on what they're really trying to do with it, what doesn't work, and what we need to change.

And the hardest part: We need to get their feedback, the positive and the negative. It hurts when people aren't satisfied; it feels like they're telling us we're stupid and worthless. We need to get over it so we can figure out how to get to hell yes. We will lose sleep for a night or two when we get negative feedback. But when we avoid getting feedback, we wind up losing sleep for months upon realizing that nobody is successful with our product and we don't really understand why and we could have figured this out and prevented it if we'd just grown a backbone and asked earlier.

Customer feedback—whether it's potential customers not buying presale or actual customers canceling postsale, or even simply raising their eyebrows in a sales conversation—helps us *debug* why we're not getting to hell yes. By relentlessly debugging what's not working, we iterate toward repeatable hell yeses. The next chapter walks through how exactly to do this.

CHAPTER 6

HOW TO DEBUG

GETTING TO HELL YES

We're working toward PULL and our repeatable "hell yes" customer success story, where customers buy as if we're irresistible and stick around as if they're addicted. How do we debug our PULL hypothesis when customers aren't saying "hell yes"?

Early on, even if we perfectly follow last chapter's sales techniques, buyers often don't buy because something about our PULL hypothesis or supply doesn't fit. It's our job to debug *why* it's wrong, try to fix it, and repeat until customers buy and say "hell yes" before and after they buy. We do this by paying intensely close attention to what buyers do and say and by trying to figure out if we need to adjust *whom* we're speaking with, the *demand* part, or the *supply* part.

My friend Rahul gives us an example of how simple and elegant this debugging process can be. He's the cofounder of a startup called 100x, which was trying to sell into technical support teams in software companies. These technical support teams get extremely detailed inquiries from their customers, for example, saying that they think they might have found an error somewhere deep in the software's advanced settings. The technical support team has to handle all of these support inquiries, and the first thing they need to do is *figure out what the hell the customer is talking about*. Tech support does this by trying to investigate the question and reproduce the error. They look across a variety of systems and tools that track user data and behavior. This process can often take up to an hour of manual investigative work per support inquiry. As a software company grows its customer base and builds more features, it has to manage more technical support requests *and* more advanced requests. The technical support team is often understaffed, which puts a significant amount of pressure on small teams to handle growing workloads.

This is where 100x fits in. They built an AI tool that automates the first round of troubleshooting for technical support requests, and gives the technical support engineer a forty-five-minute head start for each support request. Their PULL hypothesis, in theory, was a slam dunk, a no-brainer. Then they showed it to prospective customers in sales conversations.

The same thing kept happening: About halfway through the success story, the prospective customer would explain why this success story was interesting but probably wouldn't work for her company. She would say something like, "This is cool. I see how this might work for a simple application, but our software is very nuanced and complex. This couldn't possibly work in our situation." Every time, Rahul had to try to convince the customer that it actually *could* work in her situation. And while he was occasionally successful, it felt like he had to fight against a decision the customer had already made. He was pushing; the customers definitely weren't pulling. Even if he opened their minds to reconsidering trying 100x, they were extremely skeptical.

Customer objections, like customers saying, "Sorry, Rahul, our software is too complex for 100x," provide the fuel that powers our debugging process. Prospective customers are looking at our success story and saying, "That doesn't fit me." And they're explaining why it doesn't fit them. It's our job to determine exactly what they mean, and what we should change.

In Rahul's situation, there are a variety of things he could have done:

- **Change whom he is trying to sell 100x to:** Instead of talking to technical support teams at complex software companies, he could talk with companies with simpler applications.
- **Change when he tries to engage technical support teams at complex software companies:** Instead of talking to a scaling company with an already-built technical support team, he could talk to earlier-stage startups who have just hired their first technical support engineer, for example.
- **Change the words in his PULL hypothesis:** Perhaps something in the story itself was causing prospective customers to get the impression that 100x was for simple software, not complex applications.

Rahul had to decide which of these to do based on his best assessment of why these prospective customers were objecting. Rahul's hunch was that he was talking to the right potential customers and that 100x's product was a good fit for them. So by process of elimination, Rahul decided to tweak 100x's PULL hypothesis. Here's how Rahul framed 100x's success story to prospective customers:

> We do AI-automated troubleshooting for complex technical products. Most of the companies we partner with have very complex products—for example, a data company and a product analytics company. These companies are highly technical in their approach to support, which is why they've built support engineering organizations. It's not something you can just plant a simple AI system on and expect to deliver results.

When Rahul described 100x with these words, his prospective customers no longer brought up the complexity objection. In what seemed like a judo move, "complexity" went from the main reason customers didn't buy 100x to the main reason they were open to buying 100x. Prospective customers routinely said, "You know, that's exactly what I've been waiting to hear. This is exactly how I think about it; we are too complex for some simple AI tool. It sounds like your product could actually help troubleshoot our complex support requests and application."

Startups start with a PULL hypothesis and debug, debug, debug. Some startups just need to debug once to nail PULL—that's Jump's story from the last chapter. Others need many sequential debugging iterations to nail PULL—100x has since gone through many significant iterations on their path to PULL.

OFF-ROADING

Early on, there's a lot to debug. I would expect your first five or ten (or even twenty) calls to resemble a train wreck. This isn't fun, but it's how to learn.

What is likely to happen is that no matter how much research we've done, we're going to have demand, supply, and/or our target customer *very* wrong. We'll know this when we're not feeling PULL. We can call this out: "It doesn't sound like this is a project that is at the top of your priority list. What is?"

Our job in this situation is to listen intently and learn as much as possible about their to-do list. An example: An entrepreneur was trying to sell an educational technology product to schools. He was on a call with a potential customer who, upon hearing about the startup's PULL hypothesis, said, "Yeah, that is totally irrelevant to me." This was maybe five minutes into a thirty-minute call.

But the prospective customer continued: "X is irrelevant. What we're *really* trying to accomplish is Y." The entrepreneur, to his credit, didn't keep walking through X and instead had a conversation about Y, guided by the success story framework. The questions the founder asked looked like this:

- **What's the customer's project?** Tell me more about this project. What exactly are you trying to achieve?
- **Why is it unavoidable now?** Why is this your top priority right now? Of all the things you could prioritize, what's forced this to hit the top of your list?
- **What options is the customer looking into?** Which different paths are you considering?
- **Why aren't those options good enough?** What's missing in your current options?

- **Can we offer supply to fit the customer's demand?** So, if we were to offer an option that could fit the gap in your options, would that be worth exploring? Why?

This is what I call "off-roading," where our success story isn't relevant, so we instead have a structured conversation with the potential customer around their PULL, whatever it is. In this specific case, the conversation uncovered a massive business opportunity that caused the founder to evolve his success story and business in a new direction.

Your mileage might vary. You might just learn that you shouldn't talk with this kind of person anymore. Perhaps you thought you should talk to "early-stage CTOs," but it turns out that only "bootstrapped CTOs at startups with outsourced developers" have PULL. You could learn that PULL is found only in certain industries, at particular company stages, for certain job titles or seniority levels, or any other characteristic of the buyer. So you change whom you're targeting to only focus on buyers with PULL. You may realize good-fit prospective customers misinterpreted your success story, and you should reframe it so it actually makes sense to them.

And sometimes you realize *your PULL hypothesis was based on the person you wish existed, rather than a real person*—and you need to go back to the gemba to find PULL.

THE DEBUGGING SEQUENCE

While writing this book, I was also getting two companies off the ground. The first, a startup sales bootcamp, hit nearly $1 million in profit in the first year after going through three or four major debugging iterations. The second, a software company, started later and is, as I write, still in the thick of debugging. I think you'll find this in-progress journey more interesting.

The business idea came from my CTO, a friend from a previous startup. We enjoyed working together then and wanted to build a company together. We knew we wanted to bootstrap a software company instead of raising venture capital. We knew we wanted to keep the company small; neither of us wanted to manage a ton of employees. We just didn't know what the business should be. One day, he messaged me with an idea: a set of code templates that startups could use to host their software products on the cloud faster and more securely.

I started talking with potential customers about the idea. I drafted a PULL hypothesis around the project: "Deploy your software products via Amazon Web Services easily and securely." And prospective customers yawned. It wasn't their real project and certainly wasn't an unavoidable project with unworkable alternatives. Still, I pushed a few companies to use our product—which we quickly built after they agreed to pay. Of these, two companies liked it and kept using it. We asked them why they liked it, and what they said surprised us: "We had to go get a compliance audit, and your tool helped us make sure our product was ready to go through the audit much faster than it would have taken if we'd tried to do it without your product."

Interesting. Were we actually building a tool to help startups get ready for their compliance audits faster? I changed our hypothesis to: "Get your product ready for your compliance audits in minutes, not months." And as I took this to prospective customers, they were much more interested than previously. This seemed to be closer to real demand. The question was: *Does our supply fit?*

I had a series of frustrating sales conversations where prospective customers clearly had demand, but most got stuck after asking the same question: How would this impact our current product and customers? I went through a series of iterations of the success story to try to resolve this question.

When I said, "It's really easy to migrate from your current setup to ours," the word *migrate* provoked an instant and violent "Hell no!" I went through a series of similar words and concepts, and all of them performed just as poorly.

When I said, "Our product just wraps around your current setup, without any interruption," it more or less got past this objection. But it meant the product we had already built needed a massive revamp to make this promise a reality. We would likely have to invest months in product development and raise venture capital investment.

While we were iterating through the supply side, a few customers bought our product and implemented it successfully. When we compared the customers who'd been successful to those who'd objected and disappeared, we realized that prospective customers fell into two categories:

- **Category 1:** Software companies that didn't yet have customers using their product. These companies didn't have anything that we would need our product to wrap around, so they didn't have the main objection about changing systems. All the companies that bought our product fell into this bucket.
- **Category 2:** Software companies that had deployed a product, had customers, and were trying to go through the compliance audit. They didn't want to migrate to

our system and would only buy our product if it would wrap around theirs.

When we realized this, we simply stopped trying to sell to companies in category 2. We couldn't win them with our current product, so why not simply focus on companies in category 1?

As we continued to debug our PULL hypothesis, we found that we needed to change how we talked about the company and product based on those category 1 customers, and our demand and supply continues to evolve. You can see in the following table how the steps in this sequence progress.

Category	Who/When	Demand	Supply	What to Debug
1	Any startup building on Amazon Web Services	Deploy software products to the cloud easily and securely	Simple templates for building on Amazon Web Services	Didn't resonate presale; postsale people were using it differently.
2	Any startup going through a compliance audit	Get your product ready for compliance audits in minutes, not months	Migrate to our simple deployment service	Demand resonates; the word "migrate" on the supply side did not.
3	Any startup going through a compliance audit	Get your product ready for compliance audits in minutes, not months	Wrap your product with our simple compliance wrapper	Demand and supply resonate, but delivering the product would take a lot more development. The companies that bought did not need a wrapper, because they had nothing to wrap.

Category	Who/When	Demand	Supply	What to Debug
4	Startup trying to build its cloud infrastructure	Get infrastructure built for you in seconds	AI for infrastructure	TBD

By the time you finish reading this book, this might be the business, or it might have evolved further. I am starting to feel PULL in more of my sales conversations—but we'll see what happens as I continue to sell and deliver.

Something interesting happens when we change tiny pieces of our success story: We find that the story as a whole doesn't make sense anymore. For example, when we realized that our best customers were startups that hadn't yet deployed anything to customers, we realized that the way we were describing demand—"get your product ready for your compliance audits in minutes, not months"—worked decently, but it wasn't a hell yes. It didn't reflect the unavoidable project that was on their to-do list. So when we tweaked the project, we realized that they had alternatives we hadn't considered, which meant we also needed to change how we described supply for the entire success story to be a hell yes. The point? *When we debugged our customer conversations, our PULL hypothesis evolved and, as a result, so did our product and business.*

This debugging process happens in every company, at every stage. It is how we get from "an idea that works in theory but not practice" to "a business that really works, where customers pull the product out of our hands." We pay very close attention to what customers say and decide whether it's a demand problem or supply problem.

Most of the stories in this book so far have heavily featured demand debugging: MuukTest, Campground, Sparkwise, 100x. This is for three reasons. First, because demand is *upstream* of supply. If we don't clearly understand demand, how can we possibly get supply right? Second, despite demand's importance, it isn't a well-understood concept. Entrepreneurs who have historically gotten demand "right" have done so by trial and error. Third, we entrepreneurs naturally want to focus on supply without thinking about demand. I certainly am guilty of defaulting to supply-side thinking, sending hundreds of equally stupid product ideas and taglines to my patient cofounder, rather than focusing on the harsh reality of PULL. We entrepreneurs are more comfortable thinking about our product, our service, our goals. How do we make the product more compelling? How do we make it more valuable? We can make these adjustments and customers still won't care, because the problem isn't on the supply side. Remember, demand makes supply relevant. If there's no clear demand, it doesn't matter how pretty and shiny our supply is.

When debugging, how do you know if you have a demand problem or supply problem? Simply, a demand problem is misalignment with the buyer's PULL: Maybe he doesn't have a project. Maybe it's not his top priority right now. Maybe his existing options are good enough, not really unworkable.

A supply problem, on the other hand, is when a buyer has prioritized a particular project on her to-do list, but for one reason or another, your supply doesn't seem to fit—perhaps she doesn't understand your supply, or perhaps your supply actually doesn't fit her true PULL.

Here are things you'll hear from prospective customers that tell you you've got demand and supply right or wrong:

What They'll Say	Demand	Supply
When we get it right, prospective customers will say:	"What a coincidence—this is exactly what I'm focused on right now!" "We've been struggling with [options] and just didn't think anything else was available!" "It sounds like you've been listening in on our meetings!"	"Yeah, this is exactly what we need. Exactly what I was hoping for." "How do we move forward? How do I sign up?"
When we get it wrong, prospective customers will say:	"I can see how this would be useful!" "We already solved this with [option]." "I don't think this is relevant for me because . . ."	"I don't think I get it. How exactly does this work? What is it?" "How exactly are you different from [option]?" "Why does it cost that much?"

When you hear things that indicate you've got it wrong, you might need to change:

- Whom you're talking with, or when you're talking with them
- Your PULL hypothesis
- How you describe your supply
- What your supply is

Let's explore a few different debugging examples on the demand and supply sides.

DEBUGGING DEMAND

Ben started his technology company, Cobu, because of his mother. She had moved into an apartment building in a new city, and despite the building's many community spaces, she felt isolated and lonely. Ben saw his mother's struggle and decided he wanted to solve this problem. While still in school as a Harvard undergraduate, Ben started Cobu as a community and events application and service for multifamily apartments.

Years into his journey, Ben and his cofounder, Steve, seemed to be succeeding. Cobu had a few million dollars in revenue, and his customers—asset managers and property management companies of large apartment buildings—were generally happy. But on the inside, it felt like a slog. He and Steve had to work magic to close new customers and had to do a lot of convincing to retain Cobu's customers in a difficult economy—"community" was an easy line item to cut from the budget in hard times. Ben was unable to onboard new salespeople to successfully sell Cobu; it took Ben's personal story and "founder magic" to get deals done. This all meant Ben and Steve felt stuck.

As Ben tried to figure out what to do, he had hundreds of conversations with his potential buyers. He tried to understand their to-do lists and find the project Cobu's current product could fit into. He searched high and low for "community" and "resident retention" projects and couldn't find them. His customers, it seemed, almost never had this kind of demand. One blunt prospective customer told him, "Ben, if you're telling me you can improve my resident retention, I honestly don't believe you and also don't care. I've been in this business for nearly four decades, and as long as we don't actively do something stupid, resident retention always stays within a few percentage points. No matter how much money we spend or what we do, we simply don't control resident retention very much." As Ben dug deeper, he realized that this was the norm. Buyers had bought Cobu as a community perk because it seemed like a good thing to have and it wasn't very expensive. Which explained why it was so difficult for Ben to grow fast or onboard additional salespeople. That wasn't lethal when the industry was printing cash. But when the industry found itself in a downturn, every expense was increasingly scrutinized, and Cobu found itself on the chopping block.

As Ben and Steve learned more about their customers, they saw that, although customers might talk a big game publicly about community and resident retention, they spent most of their budgets on new resident acquisition. They spent money on advertising, signs, and fancy videos—you name it. Their new resident acquisition budget was at least ten times more than their resident retention budget. They were eager to hear about new, lower-cost ways to bring in new residents to fill their vacancies. Ben and Steve's conversations about new resident acquisition felt different than their conversations about resident retention and community: Buyers leaned in, pulled for more information. As the Cobu team started scoping out new products and features targeting new resident acquisition, they found it easier to start conversations. They knew they were onto something when customers started buying despite Cobu's sales pitch being described as "confusing" and their resident acquisition product idea being half-baked and delivered through spreadsheets, not software.

The second Ben and Steve iterated Cobu's success story toward resident acquisition, they tapped into buyers' real to-do lists. Previously, they had been fighting demand; Cobu was successful despite this because of Ben and Steve's sales skills and Cobu's relatively low cost. But he was playing on hard mode, and tapping into what his buyers were really spending their time and money on was the key to finding a path to, if not easy mode, less-hard mode.

We've already covered the process for debugging demand—it's the same thing Sparkwise did in Chapter 3. Find one person who pulls hard and then compare and contrast that person with others. We figure this out by focusing on what actually happens in customer conversations and firsthand observations at the gemba, not what we think might work at the whiteboard.

Some final thoughts on debugging demand. Debugging demand is particularly tricky, for three reasons:

1. **Demand exists independent of how well our conversations go.** I recall watching a founder's recorded sales call with a potential customer. By any possible measure, the call didn't go well. The founder fumbled her description of her company, and then the buyer rambled about unrelated things for most of the conversation. Oddly, a week later, the customer followed up and requested a quote. The founder had no clue what the prospective customer's project was, but that didn't mean it wasn't there. The founder just hadn't asked. I then watched the same founder flawlessly execute a sales call where the buyer didn't have any relevant demand. If you have a good conversation, you're more likely to find demand *if it's there*—but demand simply might not be there.
2. **When nobody seems to have demand, it's stressful and difficult to figure out what to do.** The solution is usually, "try to sell to more prospective customers," or, if that doesn't work, "go get a firsthand view of demand

(go to the gemba)." But even doing these things, there's no guarantee that we'll find demand. The answer, of course, isn't to stop looking for demand and instead to focus on supply. Nor is it to just assume that we will find demand someday, if our supply is "good enough" (whatever *good enough* means). I've found that the startups most effective at finding demand are the ones that do whatever it takes to hunt for it in the real world, versus those that descend into research and analysis hell. They go to the gemba and have as many one-to-one sales conversations as humanly possible—often targeting five to twenty, if not more, conversations per week—and then they debug.

3. **It is easy to see demand where it doesn't exist.** We identify a seemingly important project. Prospective customers seem excited. Then, they don't buy or take any action. The only thing that separates this "demand mirage" from real demand is payment; we often can't know if PULL is real until we get the payment notification. We have a tendency to listen with happy ears, to think that because customers say something is a big problem or an important project that demand exists. And when customers don't buy, we are shocked, bewildered, confused. The solution is to assume anything that looks like demand is fake demand until proven otherwise and to behave accordingly. Ask prospective customers skeptical questions like: Sure, sounds like this project is important, but you're probably fine doing what you're currently doing, no? Why not just use the products and services you already have? Are

> you really going to go make the case for this? Or, more simply: Is it possible for you *not* to buy this?

So yeah, it's difficult. But we can't not do it—our business only works if it fits demand.

DEBUGGING SUPPLY

Kevin is the founder of WorkStuff, a software product that is definitely not a survey tool.

"So . . . is this just a survey tool?" the prospective customer asked at minute twenty-two of a thirty-minute sales call.

Dammit, Kevin thought. It wasn't the first time he'd been asked this question. Not even the first time today. Kevin did his typical spiel: "Yeah, so, it's much more flexible than your typical survey tool, because we use AI." And, as usual, his prospective customer lost interest. She said, "Cool, thanks, yeah. It just looks like a survey tool to me, is all. I'm just not sure why I'd use it versus my existing survey tool."

Kevin's story is typical. We figure out demand, which feels like a miracle. Then we try to describe supply—and customers don't get it. We think we're a perfect fit for their demand; they think we're speaking Hungarian.

When we debug supply, we need a slightly different approach than when we debug demand. This is because debugging demand is trying to figure out PULL. When we're debugging supply, we know that a customer has PULL. We just need to make our supply *fit* their PULL.

In Kevin's case, the problem was clear: Something about how he was describing WorkStuff *caused* prospective customers *who had demand* to think, "This guy says it's not a survey tool, but it sure looks and sounds like a survey tool." When we looked at the words Kevin said and the slides he showed in his sales process, they all screamed, "This is a survey tool." Kevin showed his tool's reporting capabilities. The reports looked almost identical to the reports you'd expect from any survey tool. He showed his AI tool's four-step process: select questions, capture responses, summarize responses, and report—that is, the exact steps you'd expect to go through using a survey tool. It would have been weird if someone made it through the presentation thinking, "Wow, this is very different from a survey tool!"

So Kevin's challenge was to reframe how he described WorkStuff's supply so it couldn't be interpreted as a survey tool. As we dug into what really differentiated WorkStuff from survey tools, Kevin got frustrated and said, "Honestly, our product is closer to hiring a person to conduct a bunch of interviews than it is to a survey tool." A light bulb went off, and we changed WorkStuff's supply to be framed as "an AI interviewer." We had to replace every part of their pitch that gave the impression of a survey tool, with something that gave the impression of a human. After Kevin did this, customers never brought up the survey-tool objection again. A few months later, Kevin had closed his first $100,000 in annual revenue. As a bootstrapped solo founder, this meant he had a profitable software business—and he was just getting started.

Another friend was trying to sell AI agents to old-school manufacturers. Describing AI agents to manufacturers in 2024–2025 did not hit home. They had heard the term *AI* before but not *AI agents,* and the concept caused potential customers to stop pulling. When my friend switched out "AI agents" with the phrase "digital employees that can do specialized tasks for you," it made sense to buyers, who no longer stopped pulling at that point.

To debug your supply, listen carefully to what customers say when they are trying to understand your product and fit it into their world. They may have questions or objections. Something you've done has *caused* their questions or objections. Your job is to take their questions or objections, understand them, and reverse-engineer what you did to cause them.

This process can be used to debug every aspect of supply, all the way down to pricing. Earlier in this book, I briefly mentioned a founder whose company sells software to owners of big greenhouses. He nailed demand and supply but kept getting the same objection. Prospective customers would say, "I understand the pricing. I understand the product. It makes sense. *But how do I know it will work?* I'm taking all the risk here." Great calls would often end with this objection, and it was a coin flip as to whether the customers would buy after this. My friend initially understood this objection as a pricing problem and considered reducing his prices.

But look at the buyers' words! It's not about the pricing; it's about the risk. It's likely that they would have the same objection *no matter what his pricing was.* If he lowered his price to the point where they didn't have this objection, the price would have to be so low they probably wouldn't take his product seriously. Instead, if he offered some form of money-back guarantee, my friend could get past this objection and convert more customers, faster. (He closed a $50,000 deal *in just one call* after adding a guarantee.) The point is not that we should all add guarantees; the point is that based on customers' questions, objections, and hesitations, we can determine what parts of our supply to change.

DEBUGGING IS AWKWARD, AND NECESSARY

Our ability to debug is only as good as the inputs we get from our prospective or actual customers. When potential customers sense we're trying to pitch them or persuade them, it's often uncomfortable for them. Even if they don't feel like we're being pushy, they rarely feel comfortable giving us harsh feedback. It's socially impolite to tell someone they're ass-backward. Plus, we're very eager entrepreneurs; they don't want to rain on our parade. Maybe they're missing something, who knows. Regardless, there's nothing to gain from telling us what they really think. So they lie to us, and we take their lies as truths and spend years in the pain cave.

Here's how I solve this. My goal on a sales call is not to make a sale nor to see if my success story fits them. My goal is the exact opposite: to understand why they don't have PULL or why our supply doesn't fit them. When it doesn't fit, I find it fascinating and worth exploring.

When I was on an early sales call for my software company, I described two options my (theoretical) success story customer had: He could either do months of manual work to get his product compliant, or he could migrate to compliant software infrastructure. I asked the prospective customer, "How are you thinking about your options for getting compliant?" He said, "Yeah, we're doing it manually now. Migration . . . hadn't considered that, but that option sounds like a lot of work."

This sucked for me because my software product was the option he was saying sounded like a lot of work. At that moment, I had two options: I could have tried to convince him that migration was actually simple. Or I could have stopped the conversation there and explored why he reacted that way to the migration option. I chose the latter. He explained, "Every time I've had to do a migration, it was an awful, never-ending process. The word *migration* just makes me anxious. I don't know how annoying it is to do this compliance stuff manually, but I do know how awful a migration is, and I will avoid that like the plague." Without understanding this, I might have heard his initial hesitation and thought to describe our option as a one-click migration. But what he was really saying was, "If I see the word *migration* anywhere, my mind is closing down, and I'm sprinting in the opposite direction." Turns out, his visceral fear replicated, and I struck the word *migration* (and other similar words) out of my lexicon.

Many entrepreneurs who start out with sales are *objection-phobic* because they view objections as invalidating their PULL hypothesis and business. It is the exact opposite; objections help us understand what PULL really is, and only by seeing that reality can we build a business.

We don't get objections unless we seek them out and embrace them. Whenever we feel like we're trying to persuade someone, that's a signal that we're doing it wrong. There's something we need to fix, something that isn't working quite right. Perhaps it's our execution; perhaps it's our success story. Regardless, the feeling that we're pushing is a red flag, a signal to go back and review because something is off.

As we debug, we get closer and closer to intense, repeatable PULL. We start to scale, at first slowly and painfully, but then faster and faster. At this point, it's easy to get back into push mode—wasting a bunch of money telling everyone they should want our product. How do we avoid this and instead scale a fast-growing business that's designed around PULL?

CHAPTER 7

HOW TO SCALE

THE SUCCESS STORY FACTORY

Everything about the startup Tabs goes big and moves fast. They go from zero to $1 million in revenue in a couple of months. They raise money from top venture capitalists—$34 million in eighteen months, to be precise. Tabs's product is in a new and interesting category: It's an AI product that allows a business to upload its contracts to Tabs, and Tabs will automate invoicing, billing, collections, renewals, taxes, and so on. Tabs can serve *any business that uses contracts with its customers.* Which describes the majority of businesses on Earth.

Every startup wants to have a story like Tabs's. How has Tabs moved so fast and gone so big?

Rebecca, one of Tabs's cofounders, is, in one word, relentless. She built a routine of talking with at least three potential customers per day, every day. And she wasn't the only one. Even before they built a product, Tabs's three cofounders were *each* talking with three or more potential customers every single day.

Why do this?

"We needed to iterate our story. We needed to make sure we were building the right product. Then we needed to get users to pilot our product. Then, this became our sales process," Rebecca explains.

Tabs, I believe, has moved so fast because the cofounders look at their business in a very interesting way. They see their business as a *system* or a *factory* with the sole purpose of generating successful customers. Their job, then, is to funnel a huge volume of potential customers through their factory in order to find PULL as fast as possible. Doing this as fast as possible is what enables them to build a high-volume factory in order to grow fast and delight customers.

SEEING THE FACTORY

With PULL and the success story model, we can create a minimalist description of our business: *A factory we build to repeat a single customer success story*. A high-volume success story factory is the goal; this is synonymous with a fast-growing business.

The "success story factory" mental model winds up being extremely useful in two ways: First, it helps us visualize our business in a simple, elegant way—we can imagine the different steps in the factory, and how the factory works to repeat the customer success story. Second, using the factory mental model allows us to incorporate concepts from manufacturing to know exactly where to focus and what to fix in our business.

Our success story factory has three different steps. Together, these three steps bring customers through the process of repeating the success story. First, we need to meet someone who has the same PULL as our success story customer. Second, she needs to buy our product or service. And third, she needs to get to hell yes after she purchases when we deliver the same supply as we did with our success story customer.

Our business is a factory designed around these three steps. To name them:

1. **Pipeline:** Find potential customers.
2. **Sales:** Turn potential customers into actual customers.
3. **Delivery:** Turn actual customers into "hell yes" customers.

Tool	The Repeatable Success Story	The Success Story Factory
What it is	Why, what, and when one customer buys from us	How we repeat the success story
Components	• Demand (PULL) • Supply	• Pipeline • Sales • Delivery

PULL and the factory are tightly interlinked: If buyers have PULL, they *pull themselves* through each factory step.

On the one hand, if our success story makes promises we can't deliver on, our delivery system in the factory will fail, and therefore the whole factory is defective. On the other hand, if we have a success story but no factory, we don't have a process by which we repeat the success story. We don't grow.

Our goal is to create a factory that produces a massive volume of success stories that all look essentially identical to one another. Early on, however, our factory is going to be highly defective. We struggle to talk with many prospective customers: Our pipeline system is broken. Then, prospective customers don't convert to actual customers: Our sales system is broken. Then, actual customers aren't all shouting "hell yes": Our delivery system is broken. *Life as an entrepreneur is spent debugging PULL, debugging our success story, and debugging the factory.*

Step 1: Pipeline

The first version of our pipeline system usually looks strange. That's because we know our PULL hypothesis is probably wrong.

When we are getting started, the messages we put out into the world don't work; nobody seems to want to talk with us. This is, unfortunately, where many startups die: They don't have the chance to find PULL because they can't even figure out how to get potential customers to talk with them. In other words, they can't get any volume into their factory to learn from.

The typical startup does outreach to their potential customers that looks something like this:

> Hi, Matt,
> I'd love to pick your brain about what we've built at Prelude. Do you have 15 minutes next week?
> Prelude (part of the Casa Verde and Rackhouse

VC portfolios) is software that improves cash flow and profitability by reducing excess ordering/inventory and missed sales at dispensaries.

We automate the creation of SKU-level POs filled with the products that put the most cash back into your business, fast.

Would love to hear your feedback.

Thanks,
Michael

Whether we're selling to marijuana dispensaries like Michael and Prelude, or to a consumer, salesy messaging like this almost never works. It doesn't work because we don't yet know exactly what PULL is. *Because* we don't know what their PULL is, we have no clue what message we could send to get potential customers to stop in their tracks and talk with us. So when we send this kind of messaging, nobody responds, and we're not sure what to change or why it's not working. The question is not, How do we write more compelling sales messaging for our outreach? When we're early on, it's nearly impossible to write such compelling sales messaging that it stands out in someone's already filled inbox and brain.

The problem here—the problem that all founders face, which prevents them from getting any volume into their system so they have a chance to debug toward real PULL and their "hell yes" success story—is that we are thinking about the purpose of outreach and our sales system *backward*.

We think that our job is to use our pipeline and sales systems to convince prospective customers they should want our product. In other words, we design our pipeline and sales systems for our goals, not our prospective customers' goals. This leads us to write salesy outreach messages like Michael's, above, which are totally ineffective. Remember how demand works? Prospective customers either have PULL or they don't, and this is true whether or not we exist. Our job is to find their project and see where it is on their to-do list. If it's their priority and they have bad options, we can help them get their project done. If not, then we can either try to convince them it should be their priority (and mostly fail), or for everyone's sanity, we can just reconnect when they have PULL.

This idea changes our approach to scheduling conversations with potential customers. We don't have to sell our product or service in the outreach. Instead, our job is to get potential customers to talk with us by any means necessary and then use the conversation to figure out whether they have relevant PULL or not.

Going back to Michael's outreach from above, what if he rewrote his message not to sell the product but to generate as many conversations with potential customers as possible? Here's my rewrite:

> Hi, Matt,
> Snoop Dogg invested in my company, and we thought you might find it interesting too. Would love to get you involved in some way—customer, investor, advisor, etc.
>
> Open to chat?
>
> Thanks,
> Michael

(If you're unfamiliar, Casa Verde is Snoop Dogg's venture fund. Talk about burying the lede!)

When Prelude changed their outreach message, they started scheduling a lot of meetings, because *of course* the Snoop Dogg message worked. When Michael met with prospective customers, they didn't always have demand. Prelude's pipeline, in other words, was dirty—there was a high defect rate between the "pipeline machine" and the "sales process machine" in their success story factory. To fix this, Prelude could adjust their messaging and/or whom they were targeting—but they could only figure out what to adjust and how to change it by having all these conversations.

The point? Early on, we can either have a dirty pipeline or an empty pipeline. We can debug a dirty pipeline based on the conversations we have with potential customers. But debugging an empty pipeline is impossible: When nothing works, there is an infinite number of reasons it might not be working. So: *The goal for our early pipeline system is to have a relatively high volume of customer interactions, in order to use each interaction as an opportunity to navigate from PULL hypothesis to real, repeatable PULL.*

Now, if you don't have Snoop Dogg as an investor or aren't a serial founder out of Harvard, how do you craft a message that causes people to want to talk with you? In short, I advocate messaging that conveys this: "You're cool, I'm cool (and a real person), open to chat?"

An example is: "Hey, _______, I'm working on my second company, building a kinda crazy take on [market]. Would love to get your brutally honest take, open to chat?"

I sent a message like the above to over one thousand busy entrepreneurs and got a 30 percent response rate of people willing to talk with me. Yes, part of that is because I have an interesting background. But not all of it. Every founder I've ever met has something magical in his personal story that works in sales outreach.

Depending on your target customer, different messages will resonate. The message you send to a bar owner ("Mind if I swing by and we chat over an ice-cold Bud Light?") is going to be very different from the message you send to a vice president of supply chain ("I'm a fancy startup executive who's built an expert advisory group and thought you might be a great fit for it. Open to chat?").

And if none of this works, remember: *Go to the gemba.* Stand in a mall if you have to. Go door-to-door if you have to. Go to a conference if you have to. Spend hours every day focused on scheduling a few sales calls per day. Whatever it takes to kick-start your pipeline system so you have a chance to find PULL. Otherwise, you're wasting your life.

As we figure out and debug our success story, we adjust our approach to our pipeline system so that it is high-volume, "clean," and profitable. To grow to $1 million, $10 million, and sometimes even more, startups don't necessarily need to do a million different things to generate pipeline. Many just need one scalable growth approach, such as:

- Search (e.g., advertising on Google, SEO)
- Outbound sales (e.g., cold calling, cold emailing)
- Social (e.g., advertising on Instagram, being an influencer)
- Partnerships (e.g., getting referrals from consultants)
- Events (e.g., going to industry-specific conferences)

Finding one scalable, cost-effective pipeline approach matters *after* we've figured out our one repeatable success story.

That's because the pipeline approach that works *depends* on our success story. If, for example, our success story winds up being a hell yes for VP-level buyers at Fortune 500 companies, we are likely to need a different approach to pipeline than if our success story winds up being a hell yes for racoon breeders. The best-fit pipeline approach for our business emerges based on our success story.

A friend felt bad that he didn't have enough time to do outbound sales because he was swamped with prospective customers who came by way of referrals from industry consultants. He shouldn't feel bad and instead should just lean in to referrals from industry consultants. "X works, but I want to do Y" is almost always a worse idea than "X works, so how do we do more of X?" Another friend took the latter approach: Industry conferences worked for his business's pipeline approach, so he asked, "How do we maximize our pipeline from conferences and avoid doing anything else?" Turns out, his company was able to do a lot of conferences. Enough that they were able to hire more than one hundred sales reps just to handle the pipeline from conferences before he felt like the company was maxing out the amount of money they could invest in conferences profitably. At that point, one hundred sales reps in, he decided to figure out the company's second approach to pipeline to layer atop events. Most founders, by contrast, try to master forty different things at once. No wonder nothing works.

My mental model for the way to think about pipeline: It's like placing a toll booth. Imagine you've been granted the authority to place a toll booth anywhere on Earth. Where would you put it? Well, obviously, you wouldn't put it in a field in northern Siberia. You'd put it wherever there's a ton of traffic! Understanding *when* buyers have demand is like knowing exactly where there will be loads of traffic. If buyers have demand after they've hired a particular kind of consultant, we should find a way to partner with that kind of consultant—in other words, we put our "toll booth" with these consultants, and therefore it would be weird if buyers didn't hear about us upon working with one of these consultants. Anything other than this is likely to be less effective and a waste of time. Another example of the toll booth: Let's say your target customers are startups that go through the Y Combinator accelerator program, where startups all come together in person in San Francisco for three months. You could simply put a sign outside the building's front door advertising your product. Your potential customers couldn't physically get to where they're going without seeing it.

Unfortunately, we're often told we need to be everywhere and do everything. This sounds right until we understand demand. The impulse to do a bit of everything is just a way to admit that we haven't thought very hard about demand. It winds up being a way to waste a heroic amount of money.

On the other hand, before we've figured out our success story, our pipeline system simply exists to generate enough conversations with potential customers so that we can figure out who has demand, when, and what shape their demand takes. Costs don't matter, pretenses don't matter, scalability doesn't matter—what matters is volume and speed. I've even seen startups pay potential buyers $1,000 for an hour of their time. To the founders, that hour sped up their knowledge of PULL by a month—to them, it was more than worth the money. Before we've figured out our success story, *whatever it takes* is what's worth doing.

Step 2: Sales

Everybody wants a product that flies off the shelf—a product that's bought, not sold. I have always wanted to build something that customers can purchase without talking to me. They can go to my website and buy it while I'm asleep—or while I'm watching my Buffalo Bills break my heart again.

No matter whether we're selling million-dollar business software or ten-dollar stuffed wombats, no matter whether our aspiration is to build an elite enterprise sales force or have customers buy without talking to us, *our sales system should always start with one-on-one conversations.* We learn much more, much faster through sales conversations than from anything else—such as trying to decipher website data.

A sales system is designed to do three sequential things:

1. Figure out if the prospective customer has demand.
2. Figure out if our supply fits better than the prospective customer's alternatives.
3. Help the prospective customer purchase.

Do they have demand? If so, great! If not, let's learn why they don't have demand while others do. If they do have demand, great! Let's help them buy.

Before we have a repeatable success story that is a consistent hell yes, our sales system typically features two things:

1. A lot of people who don't have any demand
2. A lot of people who have demand, but their demand doesn't fit our PULL hypothesis or success story

As such, when we're not confident about our PULL hypothesis, sales conversations often go off-road, where we try to figure out *why* people don't have demand, *what* their demand is, and if our supply *could* fit. We use this to figure out what true PULL is, using the debugging process from the last chapter.

In the early days, when a buyer does have demand, our sales system to turn them into a buyer isn't smooth. We don't yet know exactly how our target customer expects to buy a product or service like ours. We typically start with a template of a two-step or three-step sales process like I outlined in Chapter 5, just so that we aren't empty-handed, but we should collaborate with buyers to figure out exactly what needs to happen so they can buy it. When there's demand and the supply fits, we are now on the same team as our buyers and should treat the buying process as a collaboration where we take as much work off their plate as possible. Early on, I've seen entrepreneurs go in person to the potential customer for the second meeting of their sales process—again, going to the gemba. This ain't cheap, but waiting months to learn something you could learn in person in a few hours is even more expensive.

Once we have confidence in our success story, we tighten our sales process so that there is less off-roading and a more prescriptive set of steps. When we know exactly what our success story is, we change our approach to the success story conversation to improve the conversion rate and speed up the process.

A friend has perfectly tuned his startup's sales process. Salespeople ask three questions at the beginning of their sales call; based on a prospective customer's response to these three questions, they know with nearly perfect certainty whether this person will buy. This startup has tuned their pipeline system so that north of *80 percent* of potential customers buy. Even more surprising is that his sales team has this conversion rate based solely on cold outreach. (Some say that a good conversion rate from meetings scheduled via cold outreach is 20 percent!)

The sales process is, eventually, designed around how our prospective customers assess fit. This happens in a variety of ways, depending on what *fit* means to them. This can include product demonstrations, product photos and videos, trials, pilots, security reviews, proposal reviews, frequently asked questions, or a million other things. Our sales system will form around how our prospective customers assess fit—not around how we want them to assess fit. Which means our sales process may need to feature multiple touchpoints over the course of months, whether or not we want it to. Or we may be able to evolve from one-to-one sales to one-to-many sales—such as group webinars. We might even evolve to fully self-serve sales, where buyers do their own research on our website or elsewhere and swipe their credit card without ever talking to us. We could also evolve to a model where they use our product without paying and level up to a paid version. As we figure out our success story, the answer tends to become clear. But until we figure out our success story, trying to dictate our sales process is putting the cart before the horse. All depends on the success story.

Just like with the pipeline system, our early sales system will be highly defective. It will probably be cost ineffective, where we might be meeting with prospective customers multiple times (or flying out to meet them in person) for them to make a $100 purchase decision. Obviously, this won't work forever, but that's not the point: The point is for us to learn what our repeatable success story is, as quickly as possible. These conversations with prospective customers are invaluable.

Step 3: Delivery

Getting early customers is often so difficult that we forget: Nothing matters unless we get customers to hell yes after they've purchased! The delivery process includes everything we do to get customers to hell yes after they've purchased so they renew, upgrade, and/or tell their friends about us. It is, in other words, how we repeat the success story.

In Chapter 3, I described the retention software my startup built for fast-food restaurants. It texted and emailed their employees surveys after the employees were hired and flagged which employees were at risk of quitting, so the employer could intervene.

When employers used it, they loved it. But we had, for a few months, a difficult time getting them set up. Employers took weeks to figure out the surveys they wanted to send to employees, struggling to determine the questions they should ask: Should they send question A or question B? On day seven or day fourteen? What exact wording was best?

As a result, we started to accumulate a backlog of customers who had purchased the software but hadn't implemented it yet. The backlog made me anxious, and it wasn't fun for customers either: They felt stressed because they hadn't really thought about these kinds of surveys before, and they felt annoyed because I was prodding them ceaselessly to figure it out. This was impacting our business too: The faster we got customers to hell yes post-purchase, the faster they referred their friends and the faster we grew. If they weren't implementing our product, they weren't getting to hell yes, and our growth rate was going to suffer.

The solution? We preloaded our product with our suggested surveys, and told new customers, "We recommend starting with these, which are based on best practices we've seen across the industry. You can always update them as you go along." Customers said, "Oh, great, that's what everyone else is doing? I'll do that too." They were happier, and our backlog went to zero. Problem solved.

Delivery is about figuring out the fastest, least-error-prone path to hell yes and then building a (metaphorical) bullet train that gets customers to hell yes. It should be a foolproof system that guarantees they get to hell yes; first effective, then replicable, then efficient, then scalable.

In a startup, there are always a million things about the product and postpurchase experience that could theoretically be improved. What actually moves the needle? Figuring out what the repeatable hell yes is, then making sure we fix anything preventing new customers from getting to hell yes.

When do your customers become "hell yes" customers? There is a point at which the question mark in the back of the customer's mind—*Will this actually work? Is it worth it?*—disappears. Remember, when buyers need to change, they are in *disequilibrium*. When they reach hell yes, they are in a *new equilibrium as our customer and would be weird to change.*

So what is this "new equilibrium" moment for your customers? When buyers buy something, they have some sort of an image in their minds of what their life will look like when their project is complete and how that's different from their life today. This might be a crystal-clear image; it might not be. By focusing on *their project* instead of *our product* in the sales process, we typically have a good intuition for what their new equilibrium moment will be. For my startup's retention solution, for example, it was the moment they got their first notification of an employee at risk of quitting. That's the moment they felt like their project was complete—or at least, that was the moment in which they were confident their project was en route to completion.

Early on, it's quite difficult to get customers to hell yes. This happens for a variety of reasons:

- We got their PULL wrong during the sales process, or their PULL changed after they purchased.
- They had different expectations for what we were delivering—our supply—than what they actually experienced.
- We were aligned on their PULL and our supply, but we just didn't deliver (for reasons that may or may not have been knowable in advance).

This is why I typically try to get my early customers to pay: For better and worse, we want customers to be angry and upset, not indifferent, when we don't meet their expectations. We need this painful feedback in order to figure out what hell yes really is, so we can reverse-engineer what we should actually be selling and to whom. And of course, this is why we need to deliver with an all-hands-on-deck approach. Go to the gemba: Fly out to watch them struggle to use the product or service in their world and beg for constructive feedback. By delivering the wrong thing (even the thing they thought they wanted), we find signals of what hell yes really is.

When we figure out what a hell yes is, we do two things:

1. We design our delivery system to be an idiot-proof bullet train to hell yes, so every single customer gets to

hell yes and it would require a force of nature for this not to happen.
2. We revise our pipeline and sales systems so that they *only* bring in buyers who will be "hell yes" customers.

As this makes clear, *everything* we do is in service of the hell yes that happens after purchase. We design our business factory to get every customer to that moment, when customers decide they're satisfied and are going to renew, upgrade, and/or refer others.

To summarize: There's the success story, and there's the success story factory. The factory is *how* we repeat the success story, and it incorporates pipeline (how we find potential customers), sales (how we convert potential customers into actual customers), and delivery (how we turn actual customers into "hell yes" customers). We build the factory while figuring out the success story—both work together.

Now that we understand the success story factory, it's time to explore how the factory's assembly line works—how to manage it and how to scale production.

WHAT MATTERS NOW? THE FACTORY'S BOTTLENECK

In a startup, it always feels like an infinite number of things are important. Half our business is on fire at any one point in time, and the other half is highly flammable. Answering the question Which of these million things matters most? isn't straightforward. As a result, we often struggle to make progress confidently; we second-guess our priorities and always feel like there's something important we should be doing that we're not currently doing. Interestingly, the factory framework I've developed for this chapter can help us figure out exactly where to focus and why. We go from overwhelmed with tons of competing priorities to focusing on the one thing that matters most. Here's how.

Imagine a factory line with a set of machines: Each does some part of the production process and then passes the product off to the next machine down the line, until the final product comes out at the very end. We can improve any of the machines in a variety of ways. Where should we focus?

Eliyahu Goldratt came up with an elegant answer with his Theory of Constraints.[1] First, we have to focus on what the system's goal is. In our factory, what matters is maximizing the factory's output—the number of "hell yes" customers the factory produces. Then, we need to figure out which step in the process is the bottleneck. The bottleneck is, to simplify things, the slowest machine. The system's output is defined by the bottleneck. If we speed up the slowest machine, we produce more output. *If we speed up any step other than the bottleneck, we still only produce at the pace of the bottleneck.* Output doesn't increase.

A founder came to me trying to figure out what to prioritize. She was speaking with ten potential customers per week. Of these, four had demand for which her supply was a good fit. Of those, two purchased. Nearly every customer who purchased became a "hell yes" customer. She felt like there were so many places to focus. What should she do? We talked through what improvement opportunities she felt were possible at different stages in her system, and these are the results:

System	Current State	What We Could Do
Pipeline system	• Ten potential customers per week • 40% have demand for which our supply is the right fit	• Increasing number of potential customer conversations per week by 25% equals **one extra customer every two weeks** • Changing targeting so that over 75% of conversations have demand for which supply is a good fit equals **about two extra customers per week**
Sales system	• Four potential customers with demand for which our supply is the right fit • 50% conversion to actual customers	• Increasing conversion to over 75% equals **one extra customer per week**
Delivery system	• Two actual customers per week • 100% conversion	• No improvement possible here

If her goal is to maximize the number of "hell yes" customers her business produces per week, she should first focus on targeting conversations with potential customers who are more likely to have demand. That's her current bottleneck. After she does that, she can then reassess her factory to determine what the next bottleneck to attack is.

This mental model helps her do more than maximize factory output. It helps her confidence, too, because she can relentlessly focus on one improvement effort at a time, without the voice in the back of her head saying, *What if this isn't the most important thing for me to be doing right now?*

The theory of constraints also applies within our factory's subsystems, for example, within the pipeline system. A founder asked me to look at his startup's pipeline approach to figure out what to improve. He was sending LinkedIn messages to potential customers with the goal of reaching ten conversations per week. He was stuck at four conversations per week. Here were his average weekly statistics:

- Fifty LinkedIn connection requests sent
- Twelve invitations accepted
- Twelve accepted connections messaged
- Five responses
- Four meetings scheduled

He looked at these numbers and assumed that his request-to-invitation ratio was his bottleneck. But is he right? Let's break the factory down:

Step	Current State	What We Could Do
Connection request	• Fifty requests sent per week • 24% acceptance rate	• Increase connections to LinkedIn's limit of 150 per week equals **eight extra meetings per week** • Increase acceptance rate to 40% equals about **three extra meetings per week**
Message	• Twelve messaged (100% of connections) • Five responses • 42% response-to-connection rate	• Increase response rate to 60% equals **two extra meetings per week**
Meeting	• Four meetings scheduled • 80% response-to-meeting rate	• Unclear if improvement possible here

The bottleneck was, in fact, volume. He just needed to send more connection requests. That should get him above his goal of ten meetings per week. Simple.

Find the bottleneck. Attack the bottleneck. Put more volume through the system. Find the bottleneck. Attack the bottleneck. Repeat.

Here's a simple routine that forces you to do this deliberately.

THE DEBUGGING WORKSHOP

Imagine two startups: The first approaches debugging as a thing to do when they have the time to do so. They debug informally, every month or two, usually following a founder's existential crisis. The second approaches debugging as a core part of the startup's evolution. They dedicate an afternoon every week to reviewing what's working and what isn't and changing something about the startup's PULL hypothesis, whom they are showing it to, or their factory.

The first startup debugs based on memory; the second brings the founding team together to review recorded customer conversations and get to ground truth. The first leaves their debugging session with a list of things to "look into"; the second has already implemented one or more high-leverage changes by the time they leave the debugging session.

The second startup, obviously, will make faster progress. I've watched startups do this: They debug relentlessly and make a ridiculous amount of progress. Ironically, they wind up working less hard than the first startup because they stop doing things that don't work and lean in to the things that do work. The first startup is, on the other hand, the typical startup; this is how I approached debugging in my first startup. Despite going from zero dollars to $4 million in revenue in two years, we could have moved infinitely faster and avoided a boatload of awful problems had we taken debugging seriously.

I recommend a two-to-three-hour debugging session every week or two, if not *more* frequently. Early on, I recommend doing a debugging session every five sales calls. Founders hear this and initially think, *But I'm already so busy! How can I afford to dedicate this much time?* By now, I'm sure we're on the same page: How can you afford *not* to dedicate this amount of time to debugging? How can you afford to continue doing things that don't work? Debugging is the only way to get from "something that doesn't work" to "something that works." It doesn't just happen on its own.

In a rapid debugging session, founding teams come together and:

1. Focus on the single biggest bottleneck currently facing the business. We might review "factory metrics" (shown below). Examples of bottlenecks could include:
    - We aren't generating enough sales conversations per week.
    - Very few prospective customers pull in calls.
    - Prospective customers have PULL but don't understand our supply.
    - Deals stall out after one call.
    - Onboarding and delivery aren't working.
2. Review recorded customer conversations (and any other materials) live, together, using the compare-contrast methodology to get to ground truth.

3. Determine what to change and make the change right now. If the change seems like it will take weeks or months, ask yourself: What's the version of this solution we can implement by end-of-day today?

In order to run this session effectively, many teams find it useful to keep two things in mind:

Number 1: The Current State. PULL hypothesis and factory metrics. This fits on one page (e.g., How many customer conversations have we had each week?).

Our PULL Hypothesis: Based on [Insert Person]				
Demand (PULL)				Supply
What is the **Project** on their to-do list?	Why is this project **Unavoidable**?	What **List** of options do they consider?	What serious **Limitations** do they think their options have?	What **Supply** do we offer?
[Your answer]	[Your answer]	[Your answer]	[Your answer]	[Your answer]

Our Success Story Factory			
Who	**Pipeline**	**Sales**	**Delivery**
Who are we targeting?	How are we generating sales conversations (or leads)?	How are we converting leads to customers?	How are we turning customers into "hell yes" customers?
[Your answer]	[Your answer plus link to metrics]	[Your answer plus link to metrics]	[Your answer plus link to metrics]

Number 2: Ground Truth. A running list of customer conversations in a spreadsheet (eventually in a customer relationship management tool), using the following structure:

Name	Demand (PULL)	What Supply They Want	Outcome
Jim	–	–	–
Madison	–	–	–
Wilfred	–	–	–

We continue these debugging workshops, more or less, until we die. This isn't a bad thing because this process can be enjoyable. It is like a detective novel, where we're trying to figure out exactly who pulls what supply, when, and why—and what business factory emerges around that. We get less wrong over time if we do this well, and our business takes off as a result.

SCALING THE FACTORY AND GIVING AWAY YOUR LEGOS

As we debug our factory and put more volume through the system, we have two choices:

1. Hire people who can manage the additional volume (for example, as our pipeline system scales, we may need more sales reps).
2. Redesign the system so that it can handle additional volume or meet a financial target (for example, automating certain steps of the delivery process).

We often wind up doing a mix of both; regardless, we turn over the work that we have been doing to another person or a machine. To use a great phrase from Molly Graham, an early employee at Facebook, when we are scaling our business, we are constantly "giving away our Legos."

From Molly's classic talk: "The best metaphor I have for scaling is building one of those huge, complex towers out of Legos. . . . At the beginning, as you start to scale, everyone has so many Legos to choose from . . . they're doing 10 jobs. . . . If you personally want to grow as fast as your company, you have to give away your job every couple months."[2] In other words, Molly explains, you have to *constantly give away your Legos* and hire or delegate in order to scale.

Yet, as many founders learn the hard way, when we give away our Legos, our companies often wind up turning into calcified politburos where warring departments battle for resources and put the customer last.

There's a potent example of this, which you've probably experienced if you've ever called a company's customer support line. When companies created dedicated call centers for customer support, they did so to save money and serve customers better. The logic was straightforward: If we turn customer support into a factory, we can manage it like a factory and benefit from specialization and economies of scale. In practice, costs went way up and customer satisfaction went way down.

John Seddon's work explains why this happened in call centers, and why similar things happen in *all* companies. Seddon is an iconoclastic British consultant. His writing, particularly his 2003 book, *Freedom from Command and Control*, is criminally understudied.[3] He points out that the targets that management set to measure call center performance and productivity—for example, the volume of calls each rep took per hour—wound up breaking everything.

In two sentences, here's what happens when companies set productivity targets: "Meeting the target becomes the de-facto purpose for the agent even when it acts against the purpose of the service from the customer's point of view (to solve the customer's problem). That drives costs up because unsatisfied customers have to call again."[4]

Said simply: *Any target we set becomes the purpose of whomever we set the target for.* In school, grades are the metric; getting good grades has become the purpose of school, not learning.

How does this mechanism cause our companies to spiral out of control? Well, whenever we separate production into its component parts, we need a way to measure each part of the production process. We often hire managers and set performance metrics. These measurements become each manager's purpose, and managers wind up serving their measurements, not PULL, because why *would* they serve PULL? When there's a conflict between serving PULL and hitting some performance target they're measured against, *it would be weird if they served PULL*. The drift away from serving demand compounds as managers jockey for budget and influence; for a while, the company succeeds despite itself. Eventually, it grinds to a halt and dies, replaced by a company that, too, eventually succumbs to this entropic cycle. (The government, however, doesn't go out of business, which is why its drift seems more significant and more unstoppable than that of the private sector.)

Why, you might ask, do we set targets that aren't aligned with repeating our "hell yes" success story? Because we're so often focused on what *we* want: We want to hit next quarter's sales numbers. So we set these targets, and we often get what we want—in the short term. Sales, for example, hits its revenue targets by any means necessary, whether or not that means pushing bad-fit customers to buy or aggressively raising prices on otherwise satisfied customers. Everyone—sales, customer success, product, engineering—winds up hating each other as a result. Shouldn't be a surprise; the goal became the purpose.

I call this process *purpose drift*, where each employee's individual purpose replaces the organization's purpose, such that the organization's purpose disappears. Importantly, purpose drift doesn't happen because people are bad and selfish. It is the *natural, logical outcome* of the way we tend to separate work into its component pieces and manage it. It would be weird if this didn't happen. This is a natural entropy that emerges everywhere work gets separated into departments and processes, whether that work happens on factory floors or on the internet.

I only fully grasped purpose drift when I went into early-stage entrepreneurship where I was responsible for finding customer demand and managing the work of serving customer demand. Only then was I able to understand what customers actually wanted, and how the different parts of our business served what customers wanted so they would pull. Even though purpose drift is most clearly seen from the executive's chair, its symptoms are always felt by everyone: Employees wonder why they hit their goals but the company isn't doing well, or why the sales and marketing departments always seem to hate each other, or why the product they wind up building isn't loved by customers, or why it feels like everybody's LARPing, or why they always seem to be implementing some newfangled goal-setting methodology.

We all run—and work in—some form of a modern factory. Everything is a production system, whether it's staffed by mustached machinists or pajama-clad programmers. But we can only understand our factory when we understand that *customers pull product out of the factory,* the factory doesn't push product out to the market. This means that understanding what customers pull and why is the prerequisite to effectively running or managing any single part of the factory. Purpose drift happens because we've separated work in such a way that prevents our employees from understanding customer demand and then incentivized them in ways that guarantee serving demand only happens accidentally.

Such a small thing—whether employees serve PULL or not—is the difference between our ability to create beautiful things for our customers, versus our business's descent into a warring bureaucratic politburo with low customer satisfaction. Unfortunately, modern business thinking creates factories that push ugly, self-serving things onto the world.

The solution to this problem, I believe, in rough terms, has three components:

1. Every employee reports *first* to the business's customer success story and *then* to his manager. This means the customer success story gets "veto power" over what the employee does; it shapes the bounds of what's acceptable.
2. Every employee needs a *firsthand* understanding of customer demand and the success story you're serving. Require every employee to spend time selling to and/or serving customers, and make sure she understands what demand is and why it matters.
3. Avoid steering directly into the iceberg: Don't design your organization and performance metrics in a way that would make it heroic if anyone served PULL.

This doesn't imply that we should eliminate goals or departments and descend into anarchy, just that serving PULL—or repeating the success story—should be the overarching design principle for the organization, goals, and hiring. Design an organization and goals that conflict with this or hire people who don't serve the success story first (especially if their primary career goal is to manage a large team), and you'll watch everything you've worked so hard to build burn to the ground.

Because PULL and the success story are so central to our conceptions of our businesses, we can now explore the implications of PULL on how business, generally, works and what our job *really* is as founders.

PART III

IMPLICATIONS

CHAPTER 8

THE BOTTOM-UP MODEL AND THE UNFOLDING PROCESS

We find PULL. We design supply. We develop the success story. We sell and deliver to debug the success story. We debug the system that sells and delivers the success story.

That all makes sense, but it still feels like something's missing.

This is because we are generally taught, through business school, books, and popular business media, to see businesses from a particular worldview. It is the lens of venture capital investors who are trying to understand if a company will be big in ten years. It's the lens of smart founders who are trying to understand if their ideas have any potential. It's the lens of the pitch deck and the business plan competition and the classroom and the consulting firm. This lens is zoomed out very far—we can see entire industries, markets, and products over years or decades using this lens. Nassim Taleb calls this the "Soviet-Harvard illusion" or "naive rationalism."[1] Let's be kind and just call it the *top-down lens*.

THE TOP-DOWN LENS

The Top-Down Lens: Business viewed in the abstract at scale and over time based on reason and analysis.

When we're trying to understand a business at a high level, the top-down lens seems like a reasonable place to start. What are the big trends in a particular market? How has competition evolved over time? What are the different market segments the business could target over time? Why, generally, do customers choose one supplier over another? What are the gaps in the market? What is the value chain? What are the sources of power and leverage in the industry? What is the long-term product roadmap and plan? What does this business look like at scale? These things feel important to know.

The top-down lens starts from the platonic ideal of what a successful company looks like *once it's successful*: It serves a big market, fits a market gap, started in some niche, beats competitors, has a great brand, has a differentiated product, has certain financial performance metrics, serves ice cream to employees every other Thursday. The list goes on. Then the top-down lens takes these attributes and labels them "good." These are the components of successful companies, so obviously we need to consider these things when building our companies. Now that we know what good looks like, how do we get there? Well, with long checklists, analyses, logic, plans, seventy-two-step guides, you name it.

Before we became entrepreneurs, this kind of top-down approach wasn't obviously counterproductive. It served us well in our school and work lives. It even works when raising money from venture capitalists—the "best practice" investor pitch is all top-down.

This top-down approach makes sense *if* we find demand. *Unfortunately, demand can't be found by top-down analysis, and the top-down approach tends to prevent us from finding demand.* This is the default state. The business dies while "making a lot of sense."

Businesses are explained top-down after they are successful, but they are built bottom-up.

In this book, we have explored the bottom-up lens. Almost every entrepreneur's evolution seems to start with a top-down-only approach failing—and then succeeding after adopting a bottom-up approach.

THE BOTTOM-UP LENS

The Bottom-Up Lens: Business viewed from the perspective of individual real customers who pull right now.

With the bottom-up lens, we start from ground truth: Why does one real customer need to change, and what is she trying to accomplish? How can we help her in a way that she perceives to be superior to her alternatives?

We can generate everything else off of this foundation: whom else we serve, what our product or service is, how we differentiate. Because we can't see into each buyer's mind, nor can buyers express exactly what they want, we figure this out iteratively by selling and delivering something that gets less wrong over time. Our business evolves into something that we explain using the top-down lens.

Contrasting Top-Down and Bottom-Up		
Lens/Approach	**Top-Down**	**Bottom-Up**
Where it starts	Successful companies' properties (e.g., market size, product features)	Ground truth—one real customer and why they need to change
Unit of analysis	Groups and abstractions (e.g., niches, markets, personas)	Individual buyer
What we look for	Trends, market forces	PULL at the "n of 1" level
What we build	Something that generalizes, broadly serves the group's needs	Something that serves the individual
What matters	Data, logic	Anecdote, emotion
How we operate	More thinking than action	More action than thinking
Plan of attack	Plan, roadmap, experiment	Serve one customer at a time, evolve
Benefits	Decent way to explain and understand a business	Works in practice
Drawbacks	Kills us when building new things	Doesn't "make sense" to our top-down brains or sound right

Why exactly does the top-down approach fail in practice? Every chapter in this book so far has made the same contrast:

- With the top-down approach, we create a business idea that makes sense in theory and in data and then try to convince buyers they should want it. It would be miraculous if this worked. Worse, our top-down analysis prevents us from finding real demand.
- With the top-down approach, we look at customers as abstractions (for example, niches and personas), which guarantees we describe our product or service in a way that doesn't resonate with real humans.
- With the top-down approach, we assume we can validate a business in advance, through research, analysis, and logic. We delay selling, and when we do finally start to sell and deliver, we find it doesn't work, because some percentage of our research doesn't translate into what customers want. But because we've done so much research and analysis, we tend to think this is an execution problem, rather than a demand problem.
- With the top-down approach, when we run into customer indifference, we assume the answer is to do more top-down work—to go back to the whiteboard rather than to go to the gemba.

Only using the top-down approach makes it nearly impossible to build something people actually want, something that fits any real customer's demand. It prevents us from finding demand and then blinds us to it when potential customers drop hints. Which is a problem, because virtually all startup advice comes from this top-down lens. It speaks of groups, niches, personas, markets, abstractions, general problems, business logic—*not* individual customers in the real world. Focusing on these things is more likely to prevent us from finding demand than it is to reflect demand.

Demand generates everything else. It's that simple. Our business evolves as we understand demand; we understand demand as we sell to and serve customers. We figure out our repeatable success story while selling and delivering. As our business starts to work in practice, we're in a much better position to be able to tell a top-down story and craft a long-term vision that not only makes sense, but actually works.

Which is to say: We've learned entrepreneurship upside down. We need to, at minimum, be taught the bottom-up approach *alongside* the top-down approach.

NOAH AND NICK

Noah has an MBA from MIT's Sloan School of Business and is a former hedge fund analyst. Noah is also an engineer and can build his own software. He breezed through school and was wildly successful in every job and extracurricular he put his mind to. After his MBA, he decided it was time to succeed in startups.

On the other hand, we have Nick. Like Mark Zuckerberg and Bill Gates, Nick is a college dropout. Unlike Mark and Bill, Nick didn't drop out of Harvard because he had a big business idea; he dropped out of a state school because, well, he was failing. School's not for Nick. Nor is regular employment. Nick just wants to make money and work for himself. He spent his free time in high school and college on a variety of entrepreneurial ventures from hosting parties to selling stuff door-to-door. Then one day Nick realized that he wanted to build a business, not just make some cash here and there.

How are Nick and Noah going to approach their entrepreneurial ventures? In short: Nick is going to approach his startup as if the top-down approach doesn't exist; Noah is going to do the exact opposite. Let's watch this play out.

Noah, of course, starts with a ton of traditional research and analysis. He crafts a macro-level thesis of where the business opportunity is based on industry trends and competitive forces; he gains conviction in his thesis through additional research and expert conversations. Noah conducts hundreds of interviews and pulls together a group of high-powered advisors. Perhaps he raises money, perhaps he bootstraps. He, at this point, also has a thesis about which product and customer segment he should start with. It makes logical sense as a starting point: It seems underserved and in need, and it is the obvious first step on the path to Noah's vision and broader rational thesis. To validate his starting point, Noah interviews potential customers, looking for shared problems he could solve. Based on this, he builds a plan of attack to focus on one niche and one persona first so that he doesn't overextend himself. And he also builds his plan for expanding from his first niche and persona to dominate all the other niches on his path to his billion-dollar business.

Let's check in on Nick. How did he approach this new business of his? Did he create a fifty-page business plan like Noah? Did he try to envision the future in ten years? Contemplate the different market forces and technological shifts underway?

Of course not. The top-down view doesn't exist in Nick's mind. Like Noah, Nick talked with potential customers. Unlike Noah, Nick's brain isn't cluttered with a bunch of top-down analysis. He simply asks what the potential customer is trying to solve for and what she wants to buy. Nick got his first customer before Noah finished building the first version of his top-down thesis. Nick got his first customer before *even Nick* knew what product or service he was going to deliver.

Nick then quickly tried to get another customer, because he wanted more money. Nick's second, third, and fifth customers all wanted different things. Eventually, Nick got annoyed by delivering whatever each new customer asked for—too much work. He eventually asked himself, *Who's my best customer?* and just tried to find clones of that customer.

Nick's approach emerges intuitively, via trial and error. And that's the point: The bottom-up approach I've articulated throughout this book *is what we naturally do when our minds aren't polluted with a bunch of overintellectualized ideas and playbooks that make sense in theory but don't work in practice.*

On the other hand, Noah's abstractions and plans *prevent* him from finding PULL. Given his top-down view, he might not even know to look for demand at the individual level; he thinks in terms of broad markets, personas, and abstract problems. Even if he hears what demand really is, if it conflicts with his thesis and plans, he will tune it out and continue executing his plans. He'll take it as an excuse to build more product or raise more money, until the realization hits too late that he's wrong.

In other words, Noah's approach works *only if Noah's top-down view gets the bottom-up view right.* But as we've seen throughout this book, focusing on the top-down makes it almost impossible to get the bottom-up right. The top-down approach to the question What do people want? leads us to answer in abstractions, not individual customers. Our abstractions are deeply influenced by what our minds want to exist, which means we get stuck with a mental model that doesn't play out in reality.

Nick, on the other hand, starts with real demand and real supply at the individual level. His challenge is to find something that gets customers to hell yes, and then repeat it and scale it. This is still wildly difficult, of course. But the path from "this works" to "this scales" is much easier to navigate than the path from "this works in theory but not in practice" to "now it *also* works in practice."

Plus, when something works via Nick's approach, we can zoom out and analyze top-down given the bottom-up reality.

THE BOTTOM-UP CAN GENERATE THE TOP-DOWN

It feels weird to operate without much of a top-down view if you're an overthinking founder. Noah is forced to do it when his plans don't work out. And by the way, Noah's plans *didn't* work out; he *was* wrong with his first, top-down-only idea.

But to his massive credit, Noah wasn't done with entrepreneurship. He decided to pick up some consulting gigs to make money and see what real people wanted to buy. He snagged a consulting gig with an investment firm, where the client asked him to build a custom map to evaluate a potential investment. Noah delivered, and the client was thrilled. He then talked to another investment firm, described his first success story, and asked this investor if her firm ever used maps to evaluate their potential investments. "What a coincidence," she said, "We are evaluating an investment in a local auto repair chain, and we were going to try to create a map ourselves to determine where it would be attractive to open new locations. If you can do that for us, we're more than happy to pay you to take it off our plate."

As Noah delivered new maps to investors, he built a mapping tool for himself. It allowed him to pull in all sorts of data sources to create the custom map each investor asked for. Each new investor request was a chance to improve Noah's mapping tool to make sure it worked for that investor's map request, just like it had worked for all the previous investors' requests. With enough repetitions, Noah's mapping tool allowed him to create custom maps for investors with just a few minutes of effort. And customers were willing to pay thousands of dollars for each map. In time, Noah's plan is to offer a version of his mapping tool for any investor to use. Noninvestors, too, could wind up using Noah's mapping tool—or whatever Noah's mapping tool winds up evolving into as he continues to serve customers and navigate toward PULL.

This is how most startups get built in practice. The main bottleneck is finding PULL and figuring out something that works bottom-up. When a founder figures out something that works bottom-up, *the bottom-up generates the top-down*. Noah is building a mental image of:

- Who has PULL
- What his supply needs to be to fit PULL
- Which alternatives he's competing against and what their direction seems to be
- What his existing customers and potential customers are asking for and what they're frustrated with about his current supply

With this information, Noah can confidently execute today. He can also start to see the next iteration of his success story—how his current success story might evolve. And based on this, Noah can start to generate a top-down view of his business based on what actually works.

Many startup stories go like Noah's. They start with a big top-down plan. Finally, they find something that works at the bottom-up level, and their success depends on them ditching their top-down plan and executing like banshees based on what works in practice. We feel like we need the top-down view and plan; too often these safety blankets strangle us. What we need is a different way to think about how businesses come to life that satisfies our need for a bigger-picture view. Even if it can't be planned or foreseen, we need a mental model that assures us that the things we're doing bottom-up right now *could* evolve into something big.

SUCCESS STORIES EVOLVE, BUSINESSES UNFOLD

Dr. Kenneth Stanley wrote a mind-bending book: *Why Greatness Cannot Be Planned.*[2] In it, he argues against the top-down approach for generating new innovations. This is because the path to something new is, he asserts, unplannable. We can't set an end goal; we can only do *something that works right now.* Then we take a next step that also works. Once we take that step, the next step emerges, and so on. Before we know it, we're somewhere totally innovative.

A different flavor of this same thing is Gall's law, which states, "A complex system that works is invariably found to have evolved from a simple system that worked. A complex system designed from scratch never works and cannot be patched up to make it work. You have to start over with a working simple system."[3]

As I look at startups I've seen escape the pain cave and grow big, they seem to embrace the present and evolve big businesses, grand plans, and visions *after* they find demand. Popular examples include Loom and Segment, where the founders found wild success with last-minute Hail Mary ideas based on some little random thing that worked in practice. The founders abandoned their original plans and quickly crafted plans and visions based on the simple things that worked in practice. They couldn't have kept their original plans and visions because they no longer made sense in light of what worked in the real world. Mike Maples Jr., cofounder of Floodgate Capital and the original Silicon Valley seed-stage startup investor, recently shared in his book, *Pattern Breakers,* that *over 80 percent* of his fund's most impactful startups came from pivots like these, where the business wound up being entirely different from what Floodgate had invested in.

We can look at these stories and get nihilistic: Who knows, just throw spaghetti on the wall, maybe we'll get lucky. This nihilistic approach might work better than the top-down approach. But we can do better than nihilism if we understand the process of *unfolding*[4]—the evolutionary process by which things that work are generated. When we understand this unfolding process, we can obsessively focus on serving customers without getting lost in our minds about what the future holds and top-down analysis.

The unfolding process starts with our PULL hypothesis. We can envision this as the *generator* of the business: It tells us whom we serve, what they need to accomplish, whom we compete with, and what we need to deliver. Over time, through humble interactions with customers, we debug our PULL hypothesis to find real PULL and generate our repeatable success story. Even when we find our repeatable success story, things change in the market and in our product that cause us to continually make changes to it—some big, some small. As we do this, the success story evolves or unfolds in ways that we never could have predicted early on. As the success story evolves, the business that it generates changes shape. This happens in a sequence of steps we can call the *unfolding sequence*.

Each step in the unfolding sequence generates a possibility space for the next evolution step. From our current vantage point, we might be able to see a few possibilities for the next step. We certainly can't see all the potential steps down each evolutionary path we might take or the fully unfolded shape of our success story.

Everything unfolds. This book unfolded: If you read my first draft, you would never have predicted this would be the outcome. Not a single sentence has remained from the first draft (or the subsequent seven full rewrites). Yet if you read this final draft *and* my first draft, you would see hints of the final draft in my first draft. I could only see my next draft with some fuzzy clarity. At each step, with each big rewrite and little adjustment, the argument became clearer and sharper. Eventually, this draft became possible. Talking to others who have written books, built companies, created music—this experience resembles how most things come to life; we just pretend everything is planned, because that seems cooler.

Unfolding implies that we entrepreneurs can obsessively focus on figuring out our *first* repeatable success story, without necessarily needing to see ten steps into the future. When we find something that works in practice, it generates a hint of what's to come and even what the long-term future might hold. But remember, this is generated from bottom-up information about demand in practice, not just top-down theorizing at a whiteboard about how we want the world to work. And this happens at each step in the unfolding sequence; new information emerges from the gemba, and if we're looking at spreadsheets in a conference room, we'll never see it.

BUT WHAT ABOUT ELON MUSK?

In the back of our minds, we have the most audacious, controversial, and successful entrepreneur perhaps in human history, Elon Musk, and his well-documented approach to building world-changing companies like SpaceX and Tesla. For both companies, he set a massive vision and mercilessly executed it. Yes, interesting opportunities emerged as he executed that he hadn't planned. For example, Tesla's self-driving capabilities and humanoid robots might not have been part of the original plans; the same is true of SpaceX's wildly successful satellite Wi-Fi product, Starlink. But to suggest that Elon's customer success story *unfolded* over time and that *generated* his audacious vision for Tesla and SpaceX would be a heroic misreading of these companies' histories.

Some entrepreneurs simultaneously nail *both* the bottom-up and the top-down. Importantly, Elon started Tesla building the high-end Roadster, which worked because a certain kind of wealthy person had PULL to seem more stylish and environmentally friendly than everyone else. This was step 1 of Tesla's master plan. If Elon didn't design around this kind of buyer's PULL, there might not have been a step 2.

Said differently, without the bottom-up approach, we are untethered from reality. This model is necessary and sufficient for building a great company, *but legendary entrepreneurs seem able to direct the bottom-up unfolding process toward a long-term vision.* They can, in other words, constrain the opportunity space for their business's evolution; they still evolve, but certain paths are cut off due to their visions and plans. This might lead to short-term sacrifices in service of the long-term future. Most of the time when we try to do this, we simply fail to build something people actually want. That said, to build a massive company, we do have to get both the top-down and bottom-up right. But we don't necessarily need to get both right at the same time, at the company's inception. Too many founders prioritize the top-down and ignore the bottom-up. This book makes the argument that the opposite approach is less risky and that pursuing the bottom-up is necessary.

I view this book as articulating the simple, essential, bottom-up foundation to business. No matter what, *we need to find PULL and serve demand.* Demand exists in individual customers' minds and is independent of supply. There is information encoded in how buyers behave, and by observing this, we can understand demand to build better-fit supply that serves more people. We may get this right initially; if not, we can observe how customers behave at the gemba and as we try to sell and deliver, and we can iterate toward something that fits their true demand better than their alternatives. In the early stage, I prioritize the bottom-up approach—finding real demand and then generating everything else from there.

When we see the bottom-up foundation to business, it makes our very difficult jobs a little easier. It is nearly impossible to stay sane while trying to build a company when you're not sure what matters and what doesn't. When you know exactly what you're looking for (PULL), where to look for it, how to evolve toward more intense PULL, and what to do once you've found PULL—you know, more or less, what matters.

And even still, it's hard to stay sane when building a company. So I've written a short chapter on staying sane, based on the ideas from this book. I revisit this chapter every few weeks for my own sanity. Perhaps it will help yours.

CHAPTER 9

A FOUNDER'S GUIDE TO STAYING SANE

A founder struggled for years until her startup started working. She tells a funny joke: "My first startup was in the mental health space."

If you're an entrepreneur, you get the irony. Starting a mental health startup is about the worst thing anyone could do for their own mental health. The entrepreneur's brain is rarely a fun place.

Phil at the Harvard Innovation Labs saw student entrepreneurs' brains sputter and stall out as they pursued their ideas. He had a front-row seat to the mental blockers that cause smart founders to experience debilitating mental overload that prevents them from making progress.

Phil's advice is simple. He tells every student team, "I can't say very many things with certainty, but one thing I can say is that you are not perfect and your idea, simulations, and spreadsheets are also not perfect. So, stop doing those things and start engaging with your prospective customers. That's where the answers are." Teams would agree, but despite this, they would make very little progress between Phil's advising sessions. Or they would make Pyrrhic progress, like creating documents or designing their logos or creating screen mock-ups. These things didn't matter, and students admitted they didn't matter but couldn't seem to *do what mattered*. It was strange.

What was happening here? Phil asked for my opinion. I had a hunch about what was going on in these students' brains. It's the same thing that happened in my brain as a student in the i-lab: I wasn't making much progress. I wasn't doing the obvious things to figure out the business. You might have yelled at me, "Just go talk to customers!" You might have given me a thirty-seven-step guide to success that told me exactly what to do at each step. It wouldn't have mattered.

Something was happening in my mind—*invisible* to the outside world—that was preventing me from making any real progress. My hunch, when Phil asked, was that the same thing in my mind was also in his student entrepreneurs' minds, having the same paralyzing effect. I talked to student teams to see if what was going on in my head was also blocking them from making progress. Turns out, there's this unspoken thing going on in all our minds that causes us to suffer unnecessarily, indefinitely, by preventing us from taking clear action.

We are, at a high level, trying to *solve our businesses in our brains*. We attempt to craft a mental model that incorporates these and other factors:

- Which markets we will target
- Which customers we will serve
- How they will use our product or service
- How our offering will evolve over time
- How we will win against competition
- How this will become a big business

We do this because we are a certain kind of entrepreneur: The overthinking entrepreneur. (Hell, I'm so extreme on this spectrum that this book is the result of me spending years trying to make sense of how startups work!) We overthinkers need to have a mental model of how the world works *before* interacting with it. We can't seem to operate without it. Perhaps this is true of anyone who was halfway decent at school or in the corporate world, where we learned that we're supposed to do the work before the test. As Bob Moesta says, "A students don't get started until they have the answer; D students get started *because they don't have the answer.*" If you've read this far, you're definitely an overthinker too.

The best analogy I have to what is happening in founders' brains—and what modern startup advice does to us all—comes from the lore around Alexander the Great and the Gordian knot. The Gordian knot was a wildly complex knot that, in theory, nobody could untie. Alexander decided that he would be the one to untie it; so, instead of trying to untie it with his hands, Alexander took his sword and cut the knot apart.

In the overthinking founder's mind, we all have our own personal Gordian knot. Our mental Gordian knot is the riddle of how our business will work. We are used to untying knots in our brains—every previous problem we've been given, from school to work, has been a knot in our brain. With enough effort, we've been able to untie the knot, figure it out.

But getting from idea to real business is not like any of these other knots we've untied before; it's a Gordian knot. It is so big and jumbled that we can't untie it in our minds. We're not used to a knot we can't untie in our minds, so we keep trying. Because we're overthinkers, we *can't act without untying the knot.* We feel like we need to untie the knot, understand everything, have a plan that makes sense, and only then can we start to make progress.

The Gordian knot in our brains does not respond well when we get advice, either. Every social media post we read, every thirty-step innovation process we see, every startup history we read makes the Gordian knot bigger and more complex in our brains. This is why teams weren't making progress, no matter how clear and obvious it was to Phil what their next step should be. That next step, whatever it was, was adding to the Gordian knot in the students' brains rather than taking a sword to it.

Think the Gordian knot goes away once we have a real, growing business? Think again! I can report firsthand that the Gordian knot reappears at every turn for overthinking founders, saying something like, "Guess how we're going to spend the next three days? Trying to simulate forty-seven different permutations of the future based on how much money you raise two financing rounds from now!" (I don't know about you, but often the Gordian knot decides that 3 a.m. is the perfect time to start taunting me.)

Every new input adds complexity to our Gordian knot. This is what happened to me when I finally found something that worked in practice; this is why my brain broke. I needed a mental model of startups that made sense, and all the theories I'd learned conflicted with what worked in the real world. What I saw working wasn't the sword to my mental Gordian knot; it was a new input that made my Gordian knot infinitely bigger, more complex, and impossible to untie.

Instead, coming up with the central idea of this book is the sword that cut my mental Gordian knot. It is one coherent and comprehensive way to think about how our business works, how all the pieces fit together, what matters now, and what will matter in the future. With this mental model, we *get stronger* from new inputs because we know which advice is relevant versus which advice sounds right but isn't; without this, every new input makes us weaker and more confused.

CLARITY AND INTENSITY

I was talking with a founder who had built a successful startup to many millions in revenue in a few years. But then one day, seemingly out of the blue, he quit. I asked the obvious question: Why? His answer wasn't what I was expecting: His wife had divorced him. At the time, he was still in his twenties. He'd worked nonstop, not realizing the sacrifice he was making by working so hard when everything seemed important and urgent.

When you ask a founder, "How's it going?," his answer always seems to be, "Busy."

Busy with what? Everything? Why?

There have been tons of great prioritization and productivity books. A personal favorite is *The ONE Thing* by Gary Keller, which, as its title suggests, pushes us to ask, "What is the ONE thing which, by doing it, makes everything else easier or irrelevant?"[1] But this and other productivity books assume we *know* what is most important, that we have a way to prioritize, that we can separate the things that generate from those that are generated. Without some sort of mental model about how our business works, we can't really know what matters.

Everything in a startup is always on fire, to some extent. If not actively on fire, everything *could* be vastly improved. And when we have employees, they often would *love* our help. They're often overwhelmed, too, and need guidance as to how they should prioritize.

That's why the idea of the success story and the factory is so important. If we visualize our business as a factory, we can spot the factory's bottlenecks. We *could* improve anything in our business, but only a few things matter right now. While everything often seems like it's on fire, only a few things will move the business forward right now. We can let small fires burn,[2] confident that we're focusing on the fires that really matter.

Clarity on exactly what matters *right now* allows us to attack that thing with intensity, like it's a full-contact sport. It would be crazy to say that intensity and hard work aren't necessary. But these qualities are necessary, not sufficient: They need to be directed toward what actually matters. And what matters is not always intuitive *without* the success story factory mental model. Constant eighty-hour workweeks happen either because the entrepreneur doesn't know what matters, or because the entrepreneur is pushing really hard on the most important thing. I have seen more of the former than the latter: Weapons-grade LARPing that ruins lives and relationships. I have used long hours as a way to make massive progress, and I've also used long hours as a way to feel productive. Sometimes crazy hours are necessary; often they're not. Know the difference, and you'll be able to peel yourself away to spend quality time with those you love and remind them that you do, in fact, love them.

PAIN AND OBSESSION

Customers canceling hurts. Bad sales calls hurt. Operating with very little money hurts. Watching your peers get rich while you drag yourself through the pain cave hurts.

I've seen friends retreat when they get, proverbially, punched in the face. They know they are going to get punched in the face again the next time they talk to customers, so they hide. They do so with a variety of excuses: "We need to hire someone who's really good at sales." "We need to improve our product." "We need to raise more money."

These are all signs of defeat. Their company will not survive even if they hire a good salesperson or build a good product, because the founder is retreating from the necessary pain of working with customers. Retreating will come back to bite you someday. It can't succeed.

And it will also fail if we just show up for the pain. I spent months hating my life, making tons of cold calls every day. I did it because I knew I had to do it and for no other reason. Yes, this reflected discipline and pain tolerance, but it was still stupid, *because I wasn't trying to become great at cold calls*. I was just trying to get through it.

We have to *want* the pain. I've found that the only way to do this is to become so obsessed that we actually embrace the pain. I have become obsessed with finding, understanding, and serving PULL. This doesn't just put the inevitable pain into perspective, it enables me to *lean in to* the pain. I now seek it out most days. I'm less afraid of it. And perhaps because of this, I notice the pain less now.

My hope is that this book allows you to become obsessed with understanding and serving demand in your customers' worlds. You can push through the pain cave if you are obsessed enough; *obsessing over PULL might just be the only path out.*

COMPOUNDING

There's an old quote: "The most powerful force in the universe is compound interest." We typically think of compounding as a unidimensional force, with a graph that bends upward and to the right.

The process of building a startup is one of multidimensional compounding. The startup—the success story and the factory—evolves over time through the unfolding process. This starts slowly and seems to improve at a snail's pace, but remember: Improvements compound, and the business evolves into something that looks almost nothing like what it appeared to be at the beginning.

Perhaps it takes you one hundred conversations to get one customer to pay $100, and then it takes months to get the next customer. Each new customer takes a massive amount of effort to onboard and get successful. Then we realize what customers really want is X, and we've been selling and delivering Y. It is easy to look at this reality, and then look at the successful billion-dollar companies and ask yourself, "How incompetent am I? I doubt I'll ever get there." But when we realize that we're in the early stages of compounding, we just focus on getting our next customer 50 percent faster and making our next onboarding 50 percent smoother. This adds up slowly at first but massively over time. Compounding in startups doesn't just happen, though. We have to push *ourselves* relentlessly to find PULL and design our business around it.

EXISTENTIAL ANGST

A friend's startup has grown from zero to millions of dollars of revenue. He suffered for years at near zero, with a cofounder he didn't particularly like or agree with, a product that didn't work particularly well, customers that weren't particularly happy, competition that was particularly well funded, and a host of other problems. Despite all of this, he managed to brute-force his company into existence.

And he's not happy.

His biggest fear is that he hasn't built something people actually want. He views this as the wrecking ball imminently coming to knock his company down. And not without reason: His company has experienced a lot of customers canceling, and the entrepreneur can't seem to figure out why.

Another founder described it simply: "The worst feeling in the world is trying to push a product that customers don't want."

This existential dread eats away at my friend. Every time we talk, he talks about wanting to do literally anything else. Going into real estate, joining a "normal" company, even buying a small local business and running that. "Whatever I do in my next job, I just don't want this fear that I haven't built something people actually want," he says.

This fear wracked me, too, at my first startup, because I didn't have a good way to think about what buyers want. I thought they were supposed to want our product, but our product objectively sucked even at millions in revenue and a majority of customers coming from word-of-mouth referrals. I thought our product was inadequate, and that gave me a grinding anxiety that I didn't know what to do with. I channeled it toward building more, launching new products, pushing the team harder.

Paranoia and anxiety aren't necessarily bad things if they make our product better and our success story better. In my case, they didn't. They pushed me over a stress line that I never want to cross again, where I was unable to make good decisions, think straight, or sleep. Even if I hadn't been that stressed, I couldn't have made great product decisions, *because I simply didn't have a way to think about what demand and supply were.*

With the definitions of demand and supply in this book, this existential dread won't go away fully, but the unhelpful parts should. We will still deal with well-funded competitors who copy us and incumbents who want to murder us, and these things atop the massive difficulty of building something that gets customers to hell yes. That is not easy. But we now have a simple way to think about what customers are trying to achieve and how our product or service can help them get there. We stop conflating "demand" with "wanting our product," we stop thinking our job is to go out there and convince people they should want our product, and we stop believing that the way to build great-fit supply is by building a big, fancy, expensive product. We know that we can find this out at the individual-customer level and simply repeat it, versus trying to figure this out at scale, in the abstract, for everyone all at once.

But my friend brings up a good point: Why innovate if there are many other, probably easier, ways to make money? Why not acquire small lawn care businesses and roll them up into a conglomerate, and then spin them off and sell them to private equity? Or why not climb the ladder of some corporate behemoth or join some hedge fund? These are less risky ways to make money, after all.

My answer: Innovation is the thing that most closely aligns *creating new value for others* with *creating wealth for ourselves*. Yes, this is difficult and risky, almost certainly more so than other approaches. But because many other money-making approaches fail to align new value for others with what generates our wealth, we wind up with a class of purely extractive businesspeople who make *all* of us look bad.

So yes, you could make easier money elsewhere; the biggest trade-off is what you'll see in the mirror.

PURPOSE

There is a way to simplify everything we've covered in this book. It can be summarized in one sentence: *Serve customers how and when they want to be served*. Traditional startup advice is focused on everything but this: It's focused on what we want, our goals, our milestones. As we've seen, by focusing on what we want, we almost guarantee we don't find real demand and wind up pushing more than we're pulling.

Serving others is the purpose of business; making money happens as a result of this. Sometimes we get inspired by having a big mission, like going to Mars or organizing the world's information. Whether or not we have this big mission, all of business centers around this humble purpose: to serve our customers.

This might sound trite or cliche. *Serving customers? Really? Is that it? That doesn't sound big or exciting.*

But this is what it has to be. That's how entrepreneurship works. Entrepreneurship is finding a new way to serve customers. Sure, we can envision a radically different future, but if we don't find a new way to serve customers, or if we think that serving customers is beneath us, we're not going to accomplish much of anything. Of course, customers can be annoying and service can be tedious. But if we want to stay in the game a long time and create truly great things, we approach our jobs with an eye toward humbly serving customers and meeting them where they are, not where we want them to be.

Let's reexamine the book's concepts now with this service mind-set.

The concept of demand is, quite simply, a way to describe *what people want to achieve in their lives.* They could want a promotion, to get married, to get fit. Whatever it is that they deeply want, we can visualize it as a project on their to-do list, but I hope you now see how even the idea of PULL undersells what this really is. They are grasping for something in their lives. Can we help?

The concept of supply reflects *how* these customers want to be served. Can we offer something that fits their demand infinitely better than their alternatives? Something that understands their needs so deeply that they feel understood?

The success story is an encapsulation of this into one atomic, repeatable unit, based on one real person. Everything else in this book is about how to make sure we're truly serving people and then serving as many people as perfectly as we possibly can.

When we think about business this way, the bar is shockingly low. How many businesses truly serve their customers? The phrase "customer service" means, in practice, the exact opposite of its textbook definition. Big companies are organized in ways that guarantee the customer comes last. It's a shame, but their dysfunction is our opportunity.

The service mind-set doesn't just help us find PULL; it also makes the journey more worthwhile. When I think about my business and making money, I wind up making bad, selfish decisions and getting overwhelmed and anxious. When I think about the best-fit way to serve my customers, I get inspired and motivated. I suspect this is true for you and your team too.

It's easy to forget that serving others is the purpose of business. We get so pulled into what we want, so jealous of what others seem to have, that we wind up straying and getting selfish.

Remember to serve your customers, and you'll be fine.

I hope this book has served you.

ACKNOWLEDGMENTS

My main influences while navigating the pain cave and writing this book, though I have only met two of them (and some are no longer alive): Bob Moesta, Pete Kazanjy, John Seddon, David Cancel, W. Edwards Deming, Christopher Alexander, Ryan Singer, Chris Spiek, Nassim Taleb, Eliyahu M. Goldratt, Eric Ries, Rob Fitzpatrick, Marc Andreessen, Peter Drucker, Molly Graham, Derek Sivers, Mark Rippetoe, Joe Norman, Mark Roberge, Lou Shipley, Frank Cespedes, Kenneth Stanley, John Gall, Mike Maples Jr., Ben Thompson, and Clayton Christensen.

The people whose stories made this book possible: Ivan Barajas Vargas, Renan Ulgade, Jack Hannah, Parker Ence, Varsha Ramesh Walsh, Phil Green, Ish Baid, Phil Dakin, Jimmy McDermott, Greg Borgulya, Sruti Bharat, Braden Weinstock, Eric Fox, Ryan Wan, Vince Jeong, Romain Levy, Ari Bader-Natal, Thilo Huellmann, David O'Hara, Justin Quall, Renato Villanueva, Rahul Kayala, Ben Pleat, Steve McLaughlin, Kevin Mannion, Rebecca Schwartz, Ali Hussein, Matt Skoro, Michael Murphy, Nathan Ohler, Nick Cianfaglione, and Noah Roberts.

Donna, Scott, and Wayne Snyder, and Grace, Angela, Allie, and Bob Strong provided feedback and inspiration. Additional feedback and inspiration were provided by Luke Citriniti, Mike Reszler, Robert Carpenter, Alexander van Orsow, Gorick Ng, Dan Piehler, Ross Lerner, Louis Grenier, Paulo Makdisse, Zach Wood, Shaan Rafiq, Charles Gritton, Mike McQuillan, Nate Schwalb, Edouard Reinach, Spencer Dennis, Jon Schechter, Nate Wilkins, Mat Rawsthorne, Sohrab Fadai, Angus Grundy, Eyla Milner, David London, Gregory Jessner, Finn Stuerenberg, Donna Todd, Alex Hoff, Shawna Dickson, Solomon Kahn, Olivier Moindrot, Lurein Perera, Adam Rodnitzky, Matt Lee, Douglas Drouillard, Amar Patel, Steve Munini, Jinoo Jain, Michelle Oh, Alex Zannos, Sebastian Fox, Luke Markham, Sesha Kadakia, Wade Anderson, Emily Choi-Greene, Faizaan Chishtie, Zachary Kimball, Josephine Bromley, Kristy Hrissa, Shanea Levin, Guillermo Salazar, Phil Thomas, Bert Ji, Leon Hergert, Walter Haydock, Rajesh Jayaraman, Mutuk Karpakakunjaram, Christopher Grittner, Daniel Grittner, Florian Reuter, Jonas Bärtsch, Nayyir Qutubuddin, Sudarshan Ashok, Abby Richter, Steve Travaglini, Jeffrey Beir, Michele Martin, and Emily Taber.

NOTES

Introduction

1. Tyler Hogge, "Let's go Jump—Advisor AI! One of the fastest growing startups in the country. Dare I say exceptional?," LinkedIn post, February 3, 2025, www.linkedin.com/posts/thogge_lets-go-jump-advisor-ai-one-of-the-activity-7292199686323507200-oSxc?utm_source=share&utmmedium=member_desktop&rcm=ACoAAAvVUq0BHtVkZVM0tuujtXmzhV-q7nc7pFc.

Chapter 1: Demand: What's on the Buyer's To-Do List?

1. Mark MacLeod, "David Cancel: Lessons from HubSpot, Drift, and Beyond," *The Startup CEO Show* (podcast), YouTube, 56 min., 52 sec., January 27, 2025, www.youtube.com/watch?v=2W1-1HL3AAo.
2. Mark Roberge, "The Science of Building a Scalable Sales Team," *Harvard Business Review*, July 12, 2012, https://hbr.org/2012/07/the-science-of-building-a-scal.
3. Mark Gibson, "Hubspot Review—HUG2010 First User Group Meeting," CustomerThink, October 8, 2010, https://customerthink.com/hubspot_review_hug2010_first_user_group_meeting.
4. "Zuckerberg: Twitter's a 'Clown Car That Fell into a Gold Mine,'" NBC 7 San Diego, November 7, 2013, www.nbcsandiego.com/news/national-international-mark-zuckerberg-called-twitter-a-clown-car-that-fe/2077980.

5. Dharmesh Shah, "Every product I've ever launched was awful in the beginning. One lesson learned: It's easy to take an awful product in which there is strong interest and make it better through iteration," LinkedIn post, January 2025, www.linkedin.com/posts/dharmesh_every-product-ive-ever-launched-was-awful-activity-7282620076002836480-qbI1.
6. Clayton M. Christensen, Taddy Hall, Karen Dillon, and David S. Duncan, "Know Your Customers' 'Jobs to Be Done,'" *Harvard Business Review,* September 2016, https://hbr.org/2016/09/know-your-customers-jobs-to-be-done.
7. Ryan Singer and Chris Spiek, "Episode 1: Feature Requests Aren't Demand," *Demand Thinking* (podcast), YouTube, 18 mins., 13 sec., July 23, 2017, www.youtube.com/watch?v=nMIZqim8iXU.
8. Design inspired by Joe Norman. See Applied Complexity Science, "History Is Not Reversible," Applied Complexity Newsletter, January 29, 2021, https://open.substack.com/pub/appliedcomplexity/p/applied-complexity-newsletter-january.

Chapter 2: Supply: What Fits the Buyer's Demand?

1. I've anonymized details for privacy's sake.
2. Peter F. Drucker, *The Practice of Management* (Harper & Row, 1954).

Chapter 4: Earning Your PULL Hypothesis

1. Todd Rose, *The End of Average: How We Succeed in a World That Values Sameness* (HarperOne, 2016). See Chapter 3 on ergodicity, which is the assumption that the average of a group is representative of a group. Ergodicity only applies when all members of the group are identical and static (which isn't the case, rendering personas counterproductive for startups).

Chapter 7: How to Scale: The Success Story Factory

1. Eliyahu M. Goldratt and Jeff Cox, *The Goal: A Process of Ongoing Improvement* (North River Press, 1984).
2. First Round Review, "'Give Away Your Legos' and Other Commandments for Scaling Startups," interview with Molly

Graham, n.d., https://review.firstround.com/give-away-your-legos-and-other-commandments-for-scaling-startups.
3. John Seddon, *Freedom from Command and Control: Rethinking Management for Lean Service* (Vanguard, 2005).
4. John Seddon, *Rethinking Regulation: A Manifesto* (Triarchy Press, 2024), https://citizen-network.org/uploads/attachment/881/rethinking-regulation-a-manifesto.pdf. This is a more extreme version of Goodhart's law, which states that "when a measure becomes a target, it ceases to be a useful measure."

Chapter 8: The Bottom-Up Model and the Unfolding Process

1. Nassim Nicholas Taleb, *Antifragile: Things That Gain from Disorder* (Random House, 2012).
2. Kenneth O. Stanley and Joel Lehman, *Why Greatness Cannot Be Planned: The Myth of the Objective* (Springer, 2015).
3. John Gall, *Systemantics: How Systems Work and Especially How They Fail* (General Systemantics Press, 1975).
4. Christopher Alexander, *The Nature of Order*, Book Two: *The Process of Creating Life* (Center for Environmental Structure, 2002).

Chapter 9: A Founder's Guide to Staying Sane

1. Gary Keller and Jay Papasan, *The ONE Thing: The Surprisingly Simple Truth Behind Extraordinary Results* (Bard Press, 2013).
2. Selina Tobaccowala, "Episode 10: Let Fires Burn," *Masters of Scale* (podcast), July 19, 2017, https://mastersofscale.com/selina-tobaccowala-let-fires-burn.

INDEX

INDEX

INDEX

Credit: *Teresa Johnson*

Rob Snyder is a serial startup founder and a fellow at Harvard Innovation Labs. He graduated from Harvard Business School and previously worked at McKinsey & Company. He is also an entrepreneur-in-residence and venture partner for early-stage venture capital funds. Snyder lives with his wife and daughter in New Hampshire.

RAISING READERS

Books Build Bright Futures

Thank you for reading this book and for being a reader of books in general. We are so grateful to share being part of a community of readers with you, and we hope you will join us in passing our love of books on to the next generation of readers.

Did you know that reading for enjoyment is the single biggest predictor of a child's future happiness and success?

More than family circumstances, parents' educational background, or income, reading impacts a child's future academic performance, emotional well-being, communication skills, economic security, ambition, and happiness.

Studies show that kids reading for enjoyment in the US is in rapid decline:

- In 2012, 53% of 9-year-olds read almost every day. Just 10 years later, in 2022, the number had fallen to 39%.
- In 2012, 27% of 13-year-olds read for fun daily. By 2023, that number was just 14%.

TOGETHER, WE CAN COMMIT TO **RAISING READERS** AND CHANGE THIS TREND.

HOW?

- Read to children in your life daily.
- Model reading as a fun activity.
- Reduce screen time.
- Start a family, school, or community book club.
- Visit bookstores and libraries regularly.
- Listen to audiobooks.
- Read the book before you see the movie.
- Encourage your child to read aloud to a pet or stuffed animal.
- Give books as gifts.
- Donate books to families and communities in need.

Books build bright futures, and **Raising Readers** is our shared responsibility.

For more information, visit JoinRaisingReaders.com

Sources: National Endowment for the Arts, National Assessment of Educational Progress, WorldBookDay.com, Nielsen BookData's 2023 "Understanding the Children's Book Consumer"